CONTENTS

INTRODUCTION

The symposium volume has dominated the history of seventeenth- and eighteenth-century crime over the last few years. Historians of nineteenth-century crime have produced general studies and monographs[1] but outside periodical literature the earlier period has been most notably featured in three well-received collections: *Albion's fatal tree* was the first to appear in 1975, confined to the eighteenth century and characterised by the shared perspective of its authors, *Crime in England 1550 to 1800* published in 1977 linked the eighteenth with the seventeenth century as did *An ungovernable people: the English and their law in the seventeenth and eighteenth centuries* which appeared in 1979.[2] This present volume is more modest in scope and in price. It consists of five papers which were presented to one of the seminars organised by the Department of Economic History of the University of Exeter which take place regularly at Dartington Hall.

1   Douglas Hay, Peter Linebaugh, John G Rule, Edward P Thompson and Calvin P Winslow, ed. *Albion's fatal tree: crime and society in eighteenth-century England* (Allen Lane, 1975); (Penguin Books, 1977); James S Cockburn, ed. *Crime in England 1550 to 1800* (Methuen, 1977); John Brewer and John Styles, ed. *An ungovernable people: the English and their law in the seventeenth and eighteenth centuries* (Hutchinson, 1979).

2   Edward Thompson, *Whigs and hunters: the origin of the Black Act* (Allen Lane, 1975) is a very important monograph but I do not regard it as primarily a study in the history of crime but as a fundamental study of the attitudes and working of society and politics in early Hanoverian England. To date no published eighteenth-century study has appeared comparable to David Philips, *Crime and authority in Victorian England: the Black Country 1835-1860* (Croom Helm, 1977).

Unlike the three major publications mentioned above, this volume carries its chronological coverage down to the mid-nineteenth century. In no area of social history have I been able to see any obvious breakpoint in 1800 or even 1815. This is evident in the history of crime. In terms of sanctions, the capital punishment based penal code largely persisted until the 1830s and in terms of popular attitudes, such activities as poaching, smuggling and wrecking were regarded as 'legitimate' at least as long.[1] As for methodology, there is no really significant improvement in the nature and availability of criminal statistics before the middle of the nineteenth century.[2]

The study of popular sexual attitudes and behaviour has moved far and fast in recent years, receiving momentum from historical demographers and historians of the family.[3] At most times illicit sex was largely a matter for the church courts, although bastardy always posed problems for poor law administration. During the Interregnum statute law took over and placed drastic sanctions, including in some cases the death penalty,

1   See John G Rule, 'Social crime in the rural south in the eighteenth and early nineteenth centuries', *Southern History,* I (1979) 135-53.

2   This is not to say that nothing of value can be done with eighteenth-century statistics. John M Beattie has demonstrated otherwise: see his 'The pattern of crime in England, 1660-1800', *Past and Present,* no. 62 (1974) 47-95.

3   See for example, Lawrence Stone, *The family, sex and marriage in England 1500-1800* (Weidenfeld & Nicholson, 1977); Peter Laslett, *Family life and illicit love in earlier generations* (Cambridge University Press, 1977) and G R Quaife, *Wanton wenches and wayward wives: peasants and illicit sex in early seventeenth-century England* (Croom Helm, 1979).

in the hands of its courts. Stephen Roberts examines
the working of this remarkable act in Devon. He
contributes both to our knowledge of how a statute was
regarded and enforced in a particular region and to our
knowledge of popular sexual attitudes and behaviour.

Avril Leadley focusses on the market place and the
people who interest her would probably be regarded as
cheats rather than criminals. Properly she draws attention
to the central role of the market place, to the problems
of its regulation by borough authorities, to the
difficulties of government in gaining acceptance for
uniform weights and measures and of the sensitivity of a
direct action inclined populace to malpractices.

Roger Wells turns his attention to the problem of
order. Crime and disturbance in the eighteenth century
took place in a society which lacked a large and
professional enough police system for the imposing of
prompt and effective control. Serious outbreaks of
disorder needed the employment of the military either in
its regular or in one of its irregular forms (yeomen
cavalry, volunteer regiments etc).[1] Concentrating on one
of the most disturbed of years, 1795, when disaffection
at home, threat of invasion from abroad and high food
prices all seriously concerned the authorities, Dr Wells
examines the problems of using the militia for crowd
control when, suffering from the same strains as the
population from which it was drawn, the loyalty of many
of its number was in doubt.

1   Of special interest in the context of the south-west is
     his article 'The revolt of the south-west, 1800-01: a study
     in English popular protest', *Social History*, 6 (1977)
     713-44.

Bob Bushaway brings together his skills as
professional historian and student of folklore and
customs.[1] This combination shows to advantage in his
account of conflict between the wood-taking habits of
forest populations and a law increasingly reflecting the
property concerns of the woodland owners. Here popular
attitudes and developing notions of property rights
clashed with as much import as in the more dramatic
confrontations characteristic of smuggling, poaching and
wrecking.

My own contribution uses sheep-stealing as a case-
study of rural crime c 1740 to 1840. All capital offences
create documentation but sheep-stealing was sufficiently
commonplace to do so to a usable extent. The paper is
exploratory: by looking at sheep-stealers I hope to
indicate something of the complexity and range of
motivations which lay behind the perpetration of criminal
acts in the countryside.

The conference at which these papers were presented
took place in January 1980. It was one of a series of
conferences on various themes in economic and social
history which have taken place usually three times a year
since 1967. Their purpose and scope have been explained
by Professor Minchinton in the preface to a recent volume
of *Exeter Papers in Economic History*. His practice in
publishing papers from the conferences has made available,
inexpensively, more than sixty pieces predominantly dealing
with the south-west. The contributors have ranged from

1   See his article 'Ceremony, custom and ritual: some
     observations on social conflict in the rural community,
     1750-1850' in Walter Minchinton ed. *Reactions to social
     and economic change 1750-1939* (Exeter Papers in Economic
     History, no. 12, 1979) pp. 9-29.

distinguished academics from internal and extra-mural
departments to gifted and dedicated 'spare-time' historians
('amateur' is much too patronising a term for the quality
of insight and information brought by contributors from
outside the universities and colleges). All who value
the general educational role of serious historical study
should recognise the value of the Exeter seminars and the
Papers. That large numbers do is evidenced by the fact
that the first five volumes have all sold out.[1]

This volume is perhaps not so regionally oriented to
the south-west as others in the series. Professor
Minchinton has justified his policy on this. Stephen
Roberts concentrates on Devon and west-country examples
form the basis of my own contribution. In any event, to
the extended area of Somerset, Dorset, Gloucestershire and
Wiltshire which Professor Minchinton suggests might be
added to Devon and Cornwall, historians of crime need to
add Hampshire, for that county was part of the Western
Circuit. In this broader area most of Bob Bushaway's
wood-stealers are to be found and some of Avril Leadley's
market cheats and of Roger Wells' disloyal militiamen.

For more than a dozen years I have been a regular
attender and occasional speaker at these conferences.
The setting of Dartington, the informal atmosphere and
the range and interest of the attenders drawn in by
Walter Minchinton's wide net make me hope I shall be
catching the train to Totnes for many more years yet.
I think I am the first person outside the Economic
History Department at Exeter to have been invited to edit
a volume in this series; and am honoured and flattered by
that distinction.

July 1982   John Rule

---

1   Walter Minchinton, preface to *Reactions to social and economic
     change* pp. 5-6.

FORNICATION AND BASTARDY IN MID-SEVENTEENTH CENTURY DEVON: HOW WAS THE ACT OF 1650 ENFORCED?

Stephen Roberts

On 10 May 1650 the Rump Parliament published 'An Act for suppressing the detestable sins of Incest, Adultery and Fornication', one of the most obviously 'Puritan' enactments of the Commonwealth. It provided that adulterers, male or female, could be hanged, even for a first offence, and that fornicators should spend three months in prison for a first offence and should die for a second. A similar fate was decreed for brothel-keepers.[1] The purpose of this essay is to examine the impact of this statute in one English county, Devon; to assess how far the spirit of the act survived its lapse in 1660. Offences against the act were tried both in the twice-yearly assizes and in the quarter sessions, both courts sitting at Exeter Castle. Evidence from the assizes being lacking, the sources used are the records of quarter sessions: the series of gaol calendars in the order books and the bundles of examinations and indictments.[2] Fornicators were imprisoned in the period between quarter sessions and the clerk of the court wrote 'for fornication' in the gaol calendars against the names of such offenders. A graph (see Appendix) has been compiled relating the number of fornication cases to prosecutions as a whole.

---

1   Charles H Firth and Robert S Rait, ed. *Acts and ordinances of the Interregnum, 1642-1660* (3 vols, Stationery Office, 1911) II, 387-59; Keith Thomas, 'The Puritans and adultery: the Act of 1650 re-considered' in Donald H Pennington and Keith Thomas, *Puritans and revolutionaries: essays in seventeenth century history presented to Christopher Hill* (Oxford University Press, 1978) pp.257-82.

2   Devon Record Office, Exeter: Devon Quarter Sessions Order Books, Quarter Sessions (QS) bundles in boxes 57-75 (1649-70).

Most convicted fornicators were recent mothers or pregnant. Fornication and bastardy were not clearly distinguishable as offences. Moreover, the pattern of legislation before 1650 had helped to blur the distinction. Fornication had not been an indictable offence in statute law. It was prosecuted in common law courts simply as a breach of the peace and it was left to ecclesiastical courts to prosecute the offence per se. Elizabethan legislation enjoined that unmarried mothers should be whipped and sent to Bridewell[1] and the 1650 act never formally annulled these provisions. Tudor statutes continued in force after 1650 as an alternative to the new act and the court clerks confirm this anomaly: 'for fornication' and 'for bastardy' were interchangeable descriptions of offenders. In conflating bastardy and fornication cases in the graph on p.12, contemporary practice is being reflected.

The graph indicates the number of fornication and bastardy cases successfully prosecuted by the Devon magistrates. Before the 1650 act and, indeed, for some time after it there was some reluctance by justices to enforce the law or participate in government. Men hesitated to be seen to support the republican regime established after the execution of Charles I. But from late 1651 the number of prosecutions brought under the new act never fell below double figures until its lapse. By 1653 sexual offences comprised 13 per cent of the total of prosecutions, by 1655 well over 30 per cent. During 1655 and 1656 local government was supervised by Major-General John Disbrowe and his commissioners. Juries were overhauled and clerics were scrutinized for

[1]   18 Elizabeth c3, 7 James I c4, s7: *The statutes of the realm* (12 vols, 1810–28) IV, pt.2.

signs of 'insufficiency' or disaffection. The 56 cases dealt with in 1655 did not, however, usher in a 'godly golden age'. The pace faltered in the following year and when it recovered it had fallen behind that of the other prosecutions. 1655 was the exception to a pattern of steady increase in cases.

Adultery cases have to be considered separately because they are few. F A Inderwick's 1891 study of the Interregnum[1] was based partly on west country sources and in the entire region he discovered only five prosecutions for adultery. An adultress whose offence was committed 'with a priest' was convicted at Taunton in 1650. There was a case at Exeter City sessions and three others at Devon assizes in 1654, 1655 and 1660. In none of these cases was the sentence recorded. Inderwick's examples may be augmented. At the Easter sessions of 1651 a man was gaoled for adultery and at Michaelmas 1655 another was imprisoned on suspicion of the offence. In 1652 a couple were in prison awaiting trial for incest (a capital offence under the 1650 act). In 1655 and 1656, Major-General Disbrowe's commissioner, Thomas Saunders, committed another three people for adultery.

In none of the above cases was the punishment of death by hanging recorded. The pattern of punishments indicates that fornication was dealt with at sessions as a misdemeanour and that the less frequently-detected offences of adultery, incest and brothel-keeping were regarded as felonies to be referred to assizes. The 1650 act was assimilated into an established judicial pattern. It is not possible confidently to aver that death was not the fate of adulterers; only that when on rare occasions adultery cases were judged in sessions, lesser

1   Frederick A Inderwick, *The Interregnum* (London, 1891) pp.34-9.

punishments were usually imposed.

To discover more about sexual offenders and their
backgrounds it is necessary to resort to the examinations
of suspects undertaken in the parishes by the justices.
Copies were delivered to quarter sessions to form the
basis of prosecutions. Of the over 250 examinations in
which fornication was an element which have survived,
only 25 to 30 were of men. The typical male examinee
vehemently denied the charges brought against him,
however improbable the denial. Before the Easter sessions
of 1656, Edmund Arscot JP examined a couple from the
West Devon parish of Germansweek whose child had been
born only four months after their marriage. The wife
confessed to fornication, the husband denied it. No
more details are given - it could be that the husband
felt aggrieved enough to bring the prosecution - for
such examinations tended to follow a fixed pattern, just
as magistrates followed a routine in their inquiries. In
most instances denial was easily made and could not be
gainsaid. The Plymouth merchant, Philip Francis,
questioned a Plymstock man in January 1657 about an
alleged sexual encounter a year before; the man denied
it and with no more evidence the case expired. To be
prosecuted successfully most fornication and bastardy
cases depended on confessions, since such a private
offence was rarely reliably witnessed by third parties.
Complex personal relationships lay behind statements to
magistrates. At Easter 1654, Robert Duke of Otterton
examined a Newton Poppleford couple. The woman confessed
to fornication but in mitigation claimed she had been
promised marriage by her partner. He vehemently denied
everything but added that he had long been pestered by
the woman in question and implied that her infatuation
for him lay behind the charge.[1]

---

[1]   QS Box 61: bundle Easter 1656, examinations, bundle Epiphany
       1657, examinations; Box 60: bundle Easter 1654, examinations.

Confessions by men were rare and the absence of corroborating evidence could prompt denials. The 1650 act itself, so savage in its scale of penalties, reflected the concern of its drafters that there should be legal safeguards against abuse by the sexually jealous or otherwise mischievous: 'No parties confession shall be taken as evidence within this act against any other but only against such party so confessing'. For the pregnant woman, deserted by her partner in the face of retributive magisterial inquiry, even her naming the father of her unborn child had no legal status as evidence.[1]

The stage of pregnancy at which female suspects came before the justices might offer insights into whether there was an organised campaign against the sexually active unmarried. Pre-marital pregnancies may have been ignored until physical appearances made delay impossible for those whose diligence was being monitored by central government. In some 58 cases the stage of pregnancy at which accused women were examined is beyond reasonable doubt. Women were invariably asked when sexual intercourse first occurred and on how many occasions thereafter, so it is possible to estimate a maximum length of pregnancy, provided that the testimony of examinees is accepted as accurate.[2] Most confessions thus obtained were given when the women were six months with child, according to their own statements, which suggests that many were examined when their pregnancies were all too visible and when they could hardly deny their condition.

1   Fith and Rait ed. *Acts and ordinances*, II, 389; for some examples of male confessions, see QS Box 60: bundle Midsummer 1655, examinations; Box 64: bundle Michaelmas 1660, examinations.

2   When the time of the first recalled act of sexual intercourse is given as over nine months before the date of interrogation the case has been abandoned in these calculations.

The number of examinations at later stages of child-carrying decrease steadily after the total of twenty examined at six months. There were eight cases at seven months, five at eight and four during the terminal month. In fact the second largest group of examinations occurred when suspects were, on their own confessions, three months pregnant. The number of cases at four and five months together amount to nine, the total at three months. At three months of pregnancy the condition is becoming apparent, certainly to the expectant mother and frequently to others. In short, it seems that pregnancy came to the attention of magistrates at fairly climacteric times during its course; when it was first detectable to the women concerned and to their immediate family or 'extended family' circle, and again when it was becoming clearly and publicly visible to a wider social group.

Nevertheless there were exceptions to the pattern of apprehension of illicitly pregnant women at later months in their conceptions. An Awliscombe woman claimed before a zealous careerist magistrate, John Tyrling, of the same parish, that she was pregnant after intercourse six weeks earlier.[1] Before the summer and Michaelmas sessions of 1660, John Champneys and John Wollocombe, two of the most vigorous hounders of fornicators and bastard-bearers that the Interregnum produced, were examining the last cases which could be prosecuted under the doomed 1650 act. (Wollocombe remained in the commission of the peace until his death in 1663 but Champneys was dismissed in 1661). Wollocombe examined a woman from Lapford, in mid-Devon, and Champneys a north Devon woman from Combe Martin who both claimed to be twelve days pregnant.[2] They were examined as likely producers of bastards, not simply as fornicators, but a bastardy case could hardly be successfully

---

1   QS Box 60: bundle Easter 1654, examinations.

2   QS Box 64: bundles Midsummer and Michaelmas 1660, examinations.

prosecuted at such an early stage. Local justices in fact realised that the future of 1650 act, like all Interregnum legislation, would be open to question at the return of Charles II. Champneys and Wollocombe were uncertain whether the 1650 act could any longer support their prosecutions. A confession of pregnancy, however, could be prosecuted under Elizabethan and Jacobean law. Ironically, the confused state of high politics was forcing justices to be more precise in making clear upon which statutes their action was founded than they had been when old and new legislation ran parallel.

Prosecutions after base children had been born averaged about three in each sessions meeting between 1649 and 1660. There was a streak of vindictive zeal running through the pragmatism. At Easter 1654 William Putt, another diligent justice, a merchant and an enemy of alehouse keepers, examined an Ottery St Mary couple whose only offence was to have had a child less than nine months after marriage. In January 1656, Christopher Savery interviewed a Revelstoke married woman whose husband she declared not to be the father of her child. John Blackmore inquired into the circumstances by which a Stokeinteignhead wife had a child three months before her marriage. Before the Easter sessions of 1653 Thomas Reynell, a young barrister, examined two married women, one from Dawlish, the other from Newton Abbot. One had allegedly had sexual intercourse six months before marriage, the other had been delivered of a child four months after her wedding. Such people were hardly guilty of 'abominable and crying sins'. The absence of supplementary testimonies from hostile witnesses suggests that they were not the victims of the elders or other inhabitants of their parishes.[1]

Confessions were a means of evading the jury system.

1   QS Box 60: bundles Easter 1654, Epiphany 1656, examinations;
     Box 64: bundle Michaelmas 1660, examinations; Box 59: mis-
     placed Easter 1657, examinations, bundle Easter 1653, examinations.

A confessor would be indicted on a 'true bill' and her case could proceed immediately to judgment. A bundle of 96 true bills, almost all the fornication cases recorded in Devon from 1655 to 1660, has survived.[1] Only about half of these cases proceeded to trial by jury and the sympathy of juries towards the suspects is evident. Three were judged guilty, twenty-seven were acquitted. Two cases of adultery were dismissed and two were postponed to assizes. With only a 10 per cent success rate at trial and with what may have been a jury reluctance to deal with adultery cases at all, the 'reformation of manners', so earnestly championed by Oliver Cromwell, could not be said to have enthused the yeomanry which comprised the jury.[2]

Those who made up the sub-structure of local government played little or no part in the prosecution of sexual offences. Wider parochial perceptions of wayward behaviour may be discerned in the testimonies of third parties who offered evidence of their neighbours' transgressions. In 1657 John Quick of Newton St Cyres heard the evidence of two ostlers who claimed to have witnessed fornication at a Topsham lodgings-house. An Ashton servant described how a man lay with three girls in the same bed but neither she nor a fellow-servant could admit they had seen any indecent behaviour. At Newton Abbot the proprietress of a lodgings-house watched over Nicholas Hayes, who was apparently ill. At 11 pm a serving-girl came into the room and while Mrs Webber was out, she got into bed with the sick man. In the morning the couple were reported to the constables as fornicators. Under examination the landlady admitted first that she had been in the room with them until five in the morning and then that she had not actually witnessed any

---

1   QS Box 63: loose bundle of indictments 1653-60.

2   Constables in Somerset did not interest themselves much in private morality: G R Quaife, *Wanton wenches and wayward wives: peasants and illicit sex in early seventeenth century England* (Croom Helm, 1979) p.50 et seq.

sexual activity.[1] A powerful element of personal, sexual
jealously could be inflamed by the mutual antagonisms of
communal life. Jealousies could be probed and found to
be the tap-root of false testimony. In January 1656 John
Searle questioned two women in connection with rumours of
fornication at an Ottery St Mary lodgings-house. Searle
was unconvinced and summoned Justinian Harris and Richard
Hull, the constables, who told him that the chief informant
had actually denied her own allegations to them. All she
had seen, apparently, was a woman's 'naked thigh'. The
informant's next-door-neighbour gave a garbled account of
how she lived next to him 'in the tyme of the troubles,
and ... hath had a bastard, that in the tyme of the troubles
there was very base order, a notorious whore living then
there who is now rotting of the pox'. For them all, the
allegations were the regrettable reminder of recent law-
lessness in Ottery. They were more interested in preserving social harmony than in allegations of sexual mis-
conduct.[2]

Testimonies could be tainted by motives of revenge
and by malicious snooping. A Bittadon woman alleged she
heard another woman declare that a third woman was pregnant.
An East Down man led a constable to a barn where they discovered a couple *in flagrante delicto* even though, on his
own evidence, before he ran for the constable they were
merely strolling through the village. Class tensions
lurked in some instances. A Yealmpton husbandman swore he
saw the village school-master and his servant copulating
in the window of his house. John Heywood of Chittlehampton,
servant to Col John Rolle, a presbyterian justice, confused

1   QS Box 61: bundle Epiphany 1657, examinations; Box 62:
     bundle Midsummer 1658, examinations. Similar cases, all
     involving servants, can be found in the examinations for
     Midsummer 1652, 1653 (Box 59), Easter 1657 (misplaced),
     Michaelmas 1659 (Box 64).

2   QS Box 60: bundle Epiphany 1656, examinations.

marital with professional responsibilities when alleging
that he had been cuckolded by one who, in his view, compounded the offence by abusing his master.[1]

It is not possible to isolate fully the individual
motives of informers. A rare example of genuine and
compelling outrage at a sin occurs in an examination from
1666, after the 1650 act had lapsed, and outrage mingles
'Puritan' mores with social tensions and the wilful pursuit
of those suspected to have broken social convention. In
the middle of October 1666, Katherine Haydon, the wife of
a Crediton labourer, was standing on her doorstep when
Symion Ballamy, a man she recognized as a Drewsteignton
yeoman, rode up to the house next door and, without dis-
mounting, kissed and spoke affectionately to Mary Frost,
who had run out to greet him. Mrs Haydon heard them agree
to meet in a fortnight's time outside Crediton, 'in order',
as she put it, 'to the satisfaction of their beastly lusts'.
Mrs Haydon managed to keep her own counsel until her husband,
Augustine, returned home that evening. He said nothing
until the fortnight elapsed and then he asked James Langaman,
the husbandman for whom he worked, to go with him to the
furse brake where the couple were to meet 'to see what the
effect would be'. On the fateful day they concealed themselves in the furse brake and waited. After a while the
couple appeared, embraced and then, in Haydon's words:

> Stept backe in the edge of the brake out of
> sight of this informant but nearer to ...
> Langaman who stood heard by in the hedge and
> came nearer to see the issue and further
> upon his oath constantly affirmeth that he
> found the said Mary layeing upon her back
> with her coates up to her middle and the said
> Symion layeing upon her body with his breeches
> aboute his heeles with his foot against a

1   QS Box 60: bundles Epiphany 1654, Epiphany 1656, Easter 1654,
     examinations; Box 59, bundle Midsummer 1652, examinations.

> furse stub .... Hereupon they ... spoke to
> the said Symion asking him whether an old
> man with one foot in the grave might not be
> ashamed of such wickednesse and thereupon
> the said Symion being astonished suddenly
> turned off her body soe as he, this informant,
> saw both there wickidnesse and saw his virile
> member come out of the body of the said Mary
> in a most bestiall and shamefull manner and
> further said that the said Symion did proffer
> to give them ... twenty shillings to conceale
> this his wickidnesse.[1]

The examining magistrate was no adherent of the 1650
act. Francis Fulford, of a county family from Dunsford,
had come afresh to government in 1661 without experience
of war, sequestration or of the Interregnum bench. Whether
the language of the deposition was that of the witnesses or
of Fulford or his clerk, it is apparent that 'Puritan' perceptions were not confined to the 1650s. But were there any
magistrates who specialised in these offences and who returned a particularly high number of examinations to sessions?
In many cases diligence in this kind of prosecution was matched
by conscientious attendance at quarter sessions. Thomas
Reynell, who came to three-quarters of all meetings between
1649 and 1660, examined twenty fornicators. William Putt
attended all but three meetings between 1652 and 1660 and
inquired into ten such incidents. John Champneys came to
nineteen sessions and examined sixteen cases. Christopher
Wood came to twelve and examined thirteen. The evidence of
crude numbers indicates that justices were more likely to
attend a sessions meeting than they were to examine a sexual
case. The champion specialist was John Wollocombe, who went
to a dozen meetings but examined thirty-one cases. Wollocombe
was typical of the supporters of the 1650 act in that he was
a presbyterian of the second rank of county gentry. Unlike

---

1   QS Box 71: bundle Epiphany 1667, examinations.

most of them (Reynell was the other exception), Wollocombe
survived in the commission of the peace in 1660.

After 1660 the pattern of examinations remained much
as before, with most cases involving a confession of
pregnancy. There were also confessions of fornication without pregnancy and the gamut of allegations of sexual mis-
behaviour, including some adultery cases.[1] But after the
Restoration, sentences to the common gaol were no longer
permissible.[2] The gaol calendar entries demonstrate this
change. In the 1650s the justices could despatch convicts
to the house of correction (for bastardy) or to the common
gaol (for offences under the 1650 act). There was less
choice after 1660. In January 1656 Robert Duke questioned
a pregnant Sidmouth woman. On the examination sent to the
court, Henry Fitzwilliam, deputy clerk of the peace, wrote:
'Mr Dukes clerk informs that his master will send her to
Bridewell therefore no bill of indictment to be drawne'.[3]
She went directly to the house of correction at St Thomas,
Exeter, without even appearing in court. This procedure
had remained a possibility for justices throughout the 1650s,
even though law reformers disapproved;[4] after 1660 it was
the usual course of action.

With an average number of 20-30 each year gaoled under
the 1650 act, it may seem surprising that magistrates preferred a more public and laborious course of action to swift
and summary despatch to Bridewell. The preference for public
action accords well with seventeenth-century notions of

1   QS Box 70: bundle Midsummer 1665, examinations; Box 69:
     bundle Epiphany 1664 (two cases), examinations.

2   Except for males refusing to obey maintenance orders in
     cases of bastardy.

3   QS Box 60: bundle Episphany 1656, examinations.

4   *Journals of the House of Commons*, VII (1651-9) 433;
     Thomas, 'Puritans and adultery', pp.279-80.

social control; godliness had to be seen to be preferred.[1]
Collective action also created a spirit of unity among Devon
magistrates which doubtless helped to preserve a measure of
unanimity during a time of rapid political change. In the
early 1650s collective justice mirrored insecurity. The
lapse of the 1650 act contributed to the development of extra-
sessional justice by reverting the treatment of offenders to
the justices singly or in pairs, a reversion which accorded
well with the general drift towards petty sessions government
and triumphant localism.

Forty-four Devon justices examined 255 sexual cases
between 1649 and 1660 and the same number inquired into 142
cases between 1661 and 1670. Because of deficiencies in the
Interregnum record, the estimate for the 1650s is a minimum;
the Restoration bench examined only 55 to 57 per cent of the
Interregnum caseload and this estimate is a maximum.

After 1660 no justices were specialists. Sir John Davy,
Sir John Chichester, baronets, and William Bogan, Esquire,
were the most zealous persecutors, each with eleven or twelve
cases to his credit. Davy was a presbyterian, Bogan an
Anglican and Chichester was certainly a royalist.[2] Only

1   Keith Wrightson and John Walter, 'Dearth and the social order
    in early modern England', *Past and Present*, no. 71 (1976) 41.
    Cromwell's major-generals were keen to ensure public interest
    in what they did; James Berry was pleased that his rough
    treatment of some Monmouth alesellers 'made a great noise':
    Thomas Birch, ed. *A collection of the state papers of John
    Thurloe Esq* (7 vols, London, 1742) IV, 545. Interest in
    market-places may be partly explained thus: Birch, ed. *John
    Thurloe*, IV, 278, 686.

2   Jack Simmons, 'Some letters of Bishop Ward of Exeter 1663-1667',
    Devon and Cornwall Notes and Queries, XXI (1940) 284; John L Vivian,
    The visitations of the county of Devon (Exeter, 1895) pp.99,
    174; Daphne Drake, 'Members of Parliament for Barnstaple 1492-
    1688', *Transactions of the Devonshire Association*, LXXII (1940)
    262; Public Record Office: PROB 11/365/16 (Bogan), 364/114
    (Chichester); Mary A E Green, ed. *Calendar of the proceedings
    of the committee for the advance of money 1642-1656* (3 vols,
    London, 1888) II, 641.

service on the Bench was a common characteristic among them.
The two most implacable Puritan prosecutors of the 1650s,
Wollocombe and Reynell, failed to maintain an interest in
these offences. Wollocombe's total after 1660 was two,
Reynell's one. At lesser levels, William Fry (nine cases
1649-60, four cases 1661-70) and Robert Duke (four cases
1649-60, five 1661-70) maintained some continuity in performance. For Wollocombe and Reynell a moral code had been the
outward sign of a political commitment and the Restoration
made enforcement of this code no longer practicable since
conspicuous zeal in this area would have singled them out as
unrepentant partisans of a disgraced regime. The confidence
of their erstwhile preoccupations was irrevocably lost and
their energies were diverted elsewhere rather than into an
effort to adapt their moral vision to the prevailing legis-
lative order.

To summarise briefly. The 1650 act offered magistrates
a more public method of dealing with sexual offences than had
early Stuart legislation. During the ten-year life of the
act prosecutions brought under it proceeded in much the same
way as they had done under older laws, until they reached
open court, and even then the old legislation ran parallel
and outlived the act. Most cases in the 1650s and 1660s involved confessing pregnant women and comparatively rarely was
evidence reliably wrung from third parties. Bastardy was
never clearly distinguished from fornication. There was no
general campaign against the unmarried sexually active, although one or two Puritan justices may be considered specialists. The magistrates took notice of the visibly pregnant
whose plight was common knowledge. There is no evidence to
suggest any interest in the enforcement of sexual morality
among those who formed the sub-structure of county government.
In the 1650s the justices acted diligently in the public mode
of quarter sessions rather than in the less laborious, more
private realms of petty sessions and personal initiative; a
preference which was partly an aspect of the 'reformation of
manners' but partly a reflection of a lack of confidence

among the Interregnum justices. The distinction between action at sessions and outside it accounts for the reduced sessions caseload after 1660 and is probably a more decisive difference between the 1650s and the 1660s than the influence of the 1650 act. Legislation aimed at intruding into semi-autonomous local communities was absorbed into patterns of local development, was swallowed up by local administrative procedures which proved hardier than centralist ukase.

APPENDIX

An Act for suppressing the detestable sins of Incest, Adultery and Fornication

For the suppressing of the abominable and crying sins of Incest, Adultery and Fornication, wherewith this Land is much defiled, and Almighty God highly displeased; Be it Enacted by the Authority of this present Parliament, That if any person or persons whatsoever, shall from and after the Four and twentieth day of June, in the year of our Lord One thousand six hundred and fifty, Marry or have the carnal knowledge of the Body of his or her Grandfather or Grandmother, Father or Mother, Brother or Sister, Son or Daughter, or Grandchilde, Fathers Brother or Sister, Mothers Brother or Sister, Fathers Wife, Mothers Husband, Sons Wife, Daughters Husband, Wives Mother or Daughter, Husbands Father or Son; all and every such Offences are hereby adjudged and declared Incest: And every such Offence shall be, and is hereby adjudged Felony; and every person offending therein, and confessing the same, or being thereof convicted by verdict upon Indictment or Presentment, before any Judge or Justices at the Assize or Sessions of the Peace, shall suffer death as in case of Felony, without benefit of Clergy: And all and every such Marriage and Marriages are hereby declared and adjudged to be void in Law, to all intents and purposes; and the Children begotten between such persons, notwith-standing any contract or solemnization of Marriage, to be illegitimate, and altogether disabled to claim or inherit any Lands or Inheritance whatsoever, by way of descent from, or to receive or challenge any Childes Portion in any Goods or Chattels of their said Parents, or any other Ancestor of such Parents.

And be it further Enacted by the authority aforesaid, That in case any married woman shall from and after the

Four and twentieth day of June aforesaid, be carnally known by any man (other than her Husband) (except in Case of Ravishment) and of such offence or offences shall be convicted as aforesaid by confession or otherwise, every such Offence and Offences shall be and is hereby adjudged Felony: and every person, as well the man as the woman, offending therein, and confessing the same, or being thereof convicted by verdict upon Indictment or Presentment as aforesaid, shall suffer death as in case of Felony, without benefit of Clergy.

Provided, That this shall not extend to any man who at the time of such offence committed, is not knowing that such woman with whom such Offence is committed, is then married.

Provided also, That the said penalty in the case of Adultery aforesaid, shall not extend to any woman whose Husband shall be continually remaining beyond the Seas by the space of three years, or shall by common fame be reputed to be dead; nor to any woman whose husband shall absent himself from his said wife by the space of three years together, in any parts or places whatsoever, so as the said wife shall not know her said husband to be living within that time.

And be it further Enacted by the authority aforesaid, That if any man shall from and after the Four and Twentieth day of June aforesaid, have the carnal knowledge of the body of any Virgin, unmarried Woman or widow, every such man so offending, and confessing the same, or being thereof convicted as aforesaid, shall for every such offence be committed to the common Gaol, without Bail or Mainprize, thereto continue for the space of three moneths; and until he and she respectively shall give security, to be taken by one or more Justice or Justices of the Peace before whom such Confession or Conviction shall be had, to be of the good behavior for the space of one whole year then next ensuing.

And be it further Enacted by the authority aforesaid,
That all and every person and persons who shall from
and after the Four and twentieth day of June aforesaid,
be convicted as aforesaid, by confession or otherwise,
for being a common Bawd, be it man or woman, or wittingly
keeping a common Brothel or Bawdy-house, shall for his
or her first offence be openly whipped and set in the
Pillory, and there marked with a hot Iron in the forehead
with the letter B and afterwards committed to Prison
or the House of Correction, there to work for his or
her living for the space of three years, without Bail or
Mainprize, and until he or she shall put in sufficient
Sureties for his or her good behavior during his or her
life: And if any person by confession or otherwise
shall be convicted of committing, after such Conviction,
any of the said last recited offences, every such second
offence shall be, and is hereby adjudged Felony; and the
person or persons so offending shall suffer death, as in
case of Felony, without benefit of clergy.

And be it further Enacted by the authority aforesaid,
That the Justices of Assize in their respective Circuits,
and the Justices of Peace in every County, at their
usual and General Sessions, are hereby authorized and
required to give in charge to the Grand Jury to enquire
of all and every the Crimes aforesaid: And the said
Justices of Assize, Justices of the Peace in their General
Sessions, and all and every Major and Justices of Peace
of any City, Borough or Town Corporate, that have power
to hear and determine Felonies at their usual Sessions,
shall have full power and authority to enquire by
verdict of twelve or more good and lawful men, within
the said respective Counties and places aforesaid, of
all and every the crimes and offences aforesaid, and
upon Indictment or Presentment, to hear and determine
the same, as in other cases of Felony, or Trespass, Any

Law, Usage or Custom to the contrary notwithstanding.

Provided, That no Attainder for any offence made Felony by this Act, shall make or work any corruption of Blood, loss of Dower, forfeiture of Goods, disinherison of Heir or Heirs.

Provided also, That it shall be lawful for any person or persons who shall be indicted for any the offences aforesaid, to produce at their respective Tryals any witness or witnesses, for the clearing of themselves from the said offences whereof they shall be so indicted: And the Justices before whom such Tryal shall be so had, shall have power, and are hereby Authorized to Examine the said Witnesses upon Oath.

Provided, That no parties confession shall be taken as Evidence within this Act against any other, but onely against such party so confessing; nor the husband shall be taken as a Witness against his wife, nor the wife against her husband, for any offence punishable by this Act.

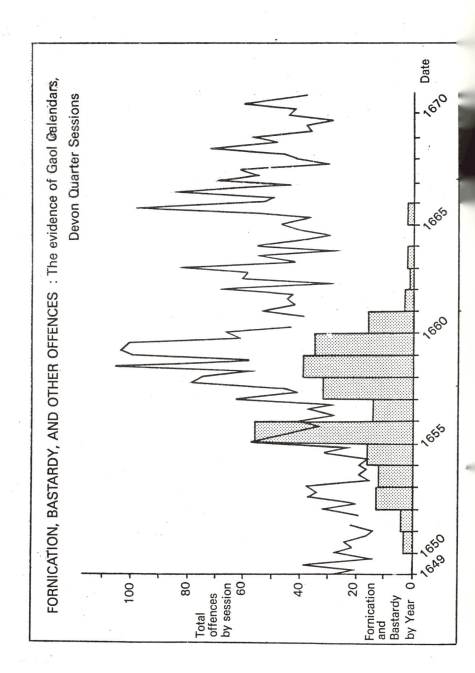

FORNICATION, BASTARDY, AND OTHER OFFENCES : The evidence of Gaol Calendars, Devon Quarter Sessions

SOME VILLAINS OF THE EIGHTEENTH-CENTURY MARKET PLACE

Avril D Leadley

We hope that the Bread in the price will abate
And Bakers remember to sell us full weight[1]

The study of the day-to-day running of the market and of
the development of notions of fair trading have been neglected
by historians, perhaps, as Professor Everitt has suggested,
because, 'with some exceptions economic history has been
written largely by men and to the ordinary unimaginative male
the importance of shopping is rarely apparent'. Yet it
would be difficult to understate the importance of the hawker,
pedlar and of the market place itself in the eighteenth century. The itinerant trader, as well as being the carrier of
purchasable goods, was the source of news and gossip for iso-
lated communities, while the market place was the hub of the
town community and, as such, the frequent stage for the expression of community grievances: 'the friction of the market
place takes us into a central area of the nation's life'.[2]

This paper examines the nefarious activities of certain
groups of traders in the south of England in the eighteenth
and early nineteenth centuries and especially of the giver of
short weight or measure and the purveyor of adulterated or
unwholesome food. In some cases extenuating circumstances
will be pleaded. The 'heroes of the piece', those market
juries and corporations who did attempt to deal systematically
and effectively with such practices, will not be treated in

---

1   'An address from the poor to the wheat hoarders, farmers, butchers,
     brewers etc' (1790), printed in Edward P Thompson, 'The crime of
     anonymity' in Douglas Hay, Peter Linebaugh, John G Rule, Edward P
     Thompson and Calvin P Winslow, *Albion's fatal tree: crime and
     society in eighteenth-century England* (Penguin, 1977) p.337.

2   Alan Everitt, *Perspectives in English urban history* (Macmillan, 1973)
     p. 5; Edward P Thompson, 'The moral economy of the English crowd in
     the eighteenth century', *Past and Present*, no. 50 (1971) 80.

the depth they deserve. The study of fraudulent trading is
an aspect of criminality which has not been accorded the
attention which it merits, while such crimes as smuggling
or sheep-stealing have occupied the foreground. In part
this reflects the availability of sources: records of the
activities of market juries are notoriously scant. It must,
however, be remarked that the bias of present day historians
of crime towards the use of Quarter Sessions and Assize
records, while it has added greatly to our knowledge of many
areas of crime, has tended to leave aside the less dramatic
criminal practices which were a major feature of market town
life.[1]

The dealer who attempted to give short weight or measure
to enhance his profit came under increasing pressure in the
eighteenth century as periodic food shortages led to a
greater suspicion of his activities as well as of those of
the farmer, miller or food dealer in general. The girth and
wealth of the publican and baker were as much an object of
bitterness as were the fine horses and pianos of the farmers:

> Me thought I saw a red-nose Oast
> As fat as he could wallow
> Whose carcase, if it should be roast,
> Would drop seven stone of tallow.
> He grows rich out of measure
> With filling measure small
> He lives in mirth and pleasure
> But poore men pay for all.[2]

In times of hardship, public sympathy was mobilised against
the sharping trader and even the country bumpkin, whose

[1]   I am grateful to my Leicester colleague Janet Grant for advice on
       this part of my paper.

[2]   'And so likewise the brewer stout/ the Chandler and the baker/
       the malt man also, without doubt/ and the tobacco taker/ though
       they be proud and stately growne/ and bear themselves so tall/
       Yet to the world it is well known/ that the poore men pay for all'
       (The poore man payes for all printed in Allan E Rodway and Vivian
       de Sola Pinto, ed., The common muse (Penguin, 1965) p. 158).

naivety in dealings was the subject of small town amusement,
became an object of the authorities' protection. The reputation of its regular traders was one of the considerations
which affected the standing of a market: a name for fiddling
could have adverse repercussions on the willingness of surrounding county people to come to it; just as could the
rumoured presence of the press gang or of disease. All would
be denied with vehemence. Not only did persistent bad practices reflect upon the efficiency of the local authorities
but they also often precipitated clashes in which the outrage
of the labouring poor could well endanger the peace of the
community. In itself, this was yet a further deterrent to
persons coming into the market.

The 'villains' fell into two main categories: those who
on a large or small scale deliberately resorted to illegal
practices in order to profit by taking advantage of inadequate
regulation, and those who were perhaps not dishonest so much
from inattention but as victims of the large degree of confusion
which surrounded the area of weights and measures in a period
when standardisation was being newly imposed over local practices. Such confusion was the subject of contemporary amusement as well as protest, as in 1818, when the *Hampshire
Chronicle* published the following anecdote:

> The measures of the publicans of a little borough
> in the West of England having lately been found
> deficient, a meeting of the Mayor and Aldermen
> took place, to consider the best means of pre-
> venting such impositions in future, when his
> worship thus addressed the court; 'I advise that
> pints and quarts used in this borough be from this
> time marked with an "H" for Ale, and "S" for cider,
> and to show that no fraud is practiced, that every
> vessel so used should first be examined by the
> proper officer and then stamped with "K" for
> corporation'.

Similar anecdotal disrespect was engendered by parliament's

1   *Hampshire Chronicle*, 14 September 1818.

attempts in 1758 to force bakers to mark their loaves with
'SW' for standard wheaten and in 1762 with 'H' for household
and 'W' for wheaten.

A parliamentary committee reported in 1758 that as a
result of the existing complex and conflicting body of legislation, the subject of weights and measures had become 'more
and more mysterious' and that the legislature faced two insep-
arable problems: the confusion resulting from centuries of
ineffectual legislation and regional variations, and the
existence of a class of traders making a living from false
dealing and drawing defence from the confusion. One of its
main recommendations was that all weights over a pound should
be made of brass, copper, bell metal or cast iron and all
below a pound of gold, silver, brass, copper or bell metal.[1]
In 1797 the market women of Winchester, having had their
wooden measures confiscated by the Market jury, procured
replacements of the same material and were reported by the
local press as not to 'have failed to employ the jackplane'
in asserting that they had as much right to 'reduce a measure'
as parliament. In the same year the market jury had seized
weights from a high street exciseman, 'merely because his
child had cut two or three ounces off each to make dumps
with'.[2]

The Carysfort Committee also recommended the adoption of
national standards of measure. In 1790 Sir John Riggs Miller,
who spearheaded demands for a complete overhaul of the system,
stated that in scarcely two counties in England was there
agreement over standard weights and measures.[3] In and around
London corn sold at nine gallons to the bushel; in other areas
at ten, eleven or even twelve. The Chester bushel contained

1   *Report from the Committee appointed to inquire into the original
     standard of weights and measures in this Kingdom*, in *Reports
     from Committees of the House of Commons, 1715-1801*, vol. II.

2   *Hampshire Chronicle*, 26 August 1797; 19 August 1797.

3   *Gentleman's Magazine*, 60 (1790) 137.

32 gallons. An attempt by the *Gentleman's Magazine* in 1767 to publish national corn prices was attacked by a correspondent from Ross (where the bushel held ten gallons) on the grounds that such a list calculated on the eight gallon bushel would seem 'a kind of trick to represent the prices of corn much lower than they really were, with a view to defeat the complaints of the people, and to show that their present murmurings for want of bread are groundless'.[1] While most attention centred on the struggle to enforce the Winchester bushel, disputes also arose over such commodities as cheese and butter. The Southampton butter dealers gained judgement in the Kings Bench for sale by the 16 ounce pound despite pleas that it had been the custom from time immemorial to deal in 18 ounces and they appeared at the following market with 'blue favours' in their hats exulting in their success. Should such considerations seem petty and unimportant, it is well to keep in mind, as Edward Thompson has observed, that 'changes in measures, like changes to decimal currency tend by some magic to disadvantage the consumer'.[2]

Such confusions gave splendid opportunities to dishonest traders. Both short-weighting and the selling of adulterated goods were common. Such and similar practices extended to every branch of retailing. A sixteenth-century ballad refers to a fishwife whose:

> ... measure is too little
> to beate the bottom out
> Halfe a Pecke for twopence
> I doubt it is a bodge
> Thus all the city over
> The people they do dodge[3]

1   *Gentleman's Magazine*, 37 (1767) 394.

2   Thompson, 'Moral economy', p. 103 and also his *The making of the English working class* (Gollancz, 1963) p. 68.

3   Cf 'The miller with his golden thumbe/ and his dusty necke/ if that he grind two bushels/ he needs must steal a peck' (*Turners dish of Lenten stuffe* (1612) in Rodway and Pinto, ed. *Common muse*, p. 191).

Prosecutions for fraudulent trading depended upon the vigilance and efficiency of local authority. The Portsmouth Corporation recorded 2876 presentments at the Court Leet for selling liquor in unsealed measures in the 18 years during 1701-21 for which records survive. In the same period 382 cases were heard for the use of unjust measures, 94 for the use of unjust weights and 18 for using a 'fixed' scale beam. While corporations were undoubtedly more active in years of dearth, prosecutions were reasonably constant in places such as Reading, Southampton and Winchester throughout the eighteenth century. More striking lists indeed than the 96 over a three month period in 1844 cited by Engels to prove the commonplace nature of trading frauds could be produced for any year in the preceding century.[1]

Most trading offences were treated as fraud under common law. The penalty usually brought with it some element of adverse publicity and the public disposal or destruction of offending produce. By the latter part of the century offenders were frequently named and castigated in the press. From at least 1780 the *Reading Mercury* was publishing names rather than veiled hints. In that year a baker of Theale was attacked in an editorial cautioning the public against buying her short-weight loaves. The woman inserted a counter-advertisement in the following issue, bringing in return no retreat from the *Mercury*: 'As for her boasted integrity and clearness of character, her neighbours might be the best judges whether it is or is not like her bread - light'.[2] Local newspapers sometimes hinted to market juries that a visitation in a particular direction might be fruitful:

> A correspondent wishes to remind the Market Jury ... that to pay some attention to the present method by which peas and beans are sold, as few of the baskets now in use ... would be found, on examination, of the standard they are estimated at.[3]

1   Frederick Engels, *The condition of the working-class in England in 1844* (Panther edition, 1969) p. 104.

2   *Reading Mercury*, 31 January, 7 and 14 February 1780.

3   *Reading Mercury*, 29 June 1789.

Papers like the *Reading Mercury* could be vehement in their denunciations:

> It is surely to be lamented that the law does not inflict a severe punishment on those unfeeling wretches who are so far lost to all sense of humanity as to omit no opportunity of imposing upon, and increasing the miseries of the poor.[1]

Once unwholesome or underweight produce was detected it was usually sold at reduced prices, destroyed or freely distributed to the poor or the inmates of the local gaol. The visitations of the market jury must have come high among the 'crowd pleasing spectacles' of the eighteenth century. In 1797 at Winchester:

> the poor people among whom the butter was distributed last week were all agog to know when the Jury Clerk was to market for them again. They were agreeably surprised with the catering of this morning. They say with such good purveyors they shall have more greasy chins than the Corporation.[2]

Shortweight or bad food force-sold by the authorities could provide material for further fraud if bought by another trader and then resold again as good:

> At a late survey of the market, I saw a man extremely solicitous to buy up a parcel of butter which by the direction of the officers, was sold much under the market price; as his appearance was neither that of a footman, or of a person who might want so much for his own consumption, curiosity led me to enquire what he was, and I was told he kept a little retail shop; my indignation was so great ... that while inquests are labouring for the good of the public, their endeavours may not be defeated by the turpitude of those who, at the very time they are witnesses of the punishment and ignominy of men convicted of using false weights, endeavour to purchase the goods thus stig-matised with a view of reaping a larger profit in retailing them to the poor.[3]

The motives behind fraudulent trading practices could be more complex than simple profiteering. What is to be made of

1   *Reading Mercury,* 1 June 1772.

2   *Hampshire Chronicle,* 26 August 1797.

3   *Hampshire Chronicle,* 14 September 1772.

the reasoning of the Southampton butcher who in 1773 preferred that a considerable quantity of beef seized by the
market jury as being rotten should be destroyed rather than
sold at a reduced price to the poor?[1] Sport, resentment
and even self-righteousness can be seen in the defence of Bob
the packman in the *Mill on the Floss* that he was an honest
man despite the practised use of his 'big thumb', which he
placed at the end of the yard before cutting a measure of
flannel to give an inch less. While agreeing to give up the
deceit, he bemoaned:

> I couldn't find another trick so good - an' what
> wd' be the use of' havin' a big thumb? it might
> as well ha' been narrow.
> ... it's them skinflint women as haggle and haggle,
> an' 'ud niver ask theirselves how I got my dinner
> out on't ... I must hev a bit of sport, an' now I
> don't go wi' the ferrets, I'd no varmint to come
> over but them haggling women.[2]

Traders more upright than Bob could fall foul of the law
through ill-luck. Weights could become light purely through
use or have been unknowingly sized to a standard different
from that currently demanded by the town authority. In 1795
Reading's Leet Jury reported that the town's own
weights, by which all the weights used in the town were sized,
had been made lighter than the Exchequer standards 'by
constant use'.[3] In 1813 the Winchester Jury discovered that
several new weights seized conformed to the Guild of West-
minster standards instead of those of the City of London,
to which the 'official' weights conformed.[4] Trouble could
come to an honest dealer who had bought deficient weights
in good faith. Edward Belson, a Reading Quaker and distiller
of undoubted rectitude, recorded tersely in his diary in 1721:

1   *Hampshire Chronicle,* 15 March 1773.

2   George Eliot, *The Mill on the Floss* (Everyman edition) p. 302.

3   Minutes of the Court Leat 1784-99: October 1795, Reading Record
     Office, T/Z 4/1 78.

4   *Hampshire Chronicle,* 1 March 1813.

on ye 21st I was fined at Wokingham for my weights
being too light (which I bott of Wm Thorborough)
6s 8d and 2s to ye Councillor Bradly.[1]

The vigilant market jury was not the only source of apprehension: the negligent or lazy trader as well as the deliberately dishonest could fall foul of 'professional' informers
who regularly seized upon such infringements of weight and
quality control as well as reporting infringements of stamp
duties. In 1816 a pair of London informers working through
Marlow, Beaconsfield and Chalfont, ordered large quantities
of small bread, explaining to the bakers that they needed
urgently to feed a great number of men. Any small deficiency in weight or failure to mark even the smallest loaf
would be seized upon and information laid. On this excursion
the pair obtained £10 penalties and £2 law expenses as a
result of one information.[2]

There were, of course, out-and-out villains even among
the outwardly pure of heart. Much amusement was caused in
Winchester in 1773 when among many fined for short-weight was
'our sanctified Methodist preacher'. This person was not,
however, easily cowed into keeping a low profile, for two
years later, after being fined again for the same offence,
he attempted to get a warrant issued against some young men
who had 'caused a disturbance' outside his meeting-house. The
magistrates refused his warrant and instead advised him to
go home and mind his own business, to desist from selling
bad weights and 'to be careful of his dealings in pewter'.[3]

On market and fair days towns would receive an influx
of those intending to defraud as well as the more easily
identified criminal element of pickpockets and confidence

1   Manuscript diary of Edward Belson, Reading Record Office, D/EZ 12 1/5.

2   *Hampshire Chronicle*, 20 May 1816.

3   *Hampshire Chronicle*, 4 October 1773, 13 March 1775.

tricksters. All sought to take advantage of bustling crowds
and full pockets; in cant terms, 'catching harvest', 'Bag
hunters', mutchers (the robbers of drunks) and snide
pitchers (passers of false drafts and coins) had a field
day. John Poulter listed eight 'knowing arts' by which
people were defrauded at markets and fairs and local
papers regularly warned against the hazards of market day
intercourse.[1]

For such tricksters the busy trading centre allowed
a high level of activity but the actions of adulterers
were more constant and more insidious. Edward Thompson
has argued that the important point is that the townspeople
believed that such practices as the adulteration of flour
with ground bones were common, even if some of the charges
made by Markham and Manning in the 1750s adulteration scandal
were suspect.[2] Deliberate and often dangerous adulteration
of foodstuffs was a commonplace of eighteenth-century life.
We are interested in deliberate action rather than in
incidental contamination such as featured in Smollett's
description of London milk: 'exposed to foul rinsings dis-
charged from doors and windows, spittle, snot and tobacco
quids from foot passengers'.[3] Alum _was_ used to whiten
bread, drugs added to porter and ale, logwood to brandy,
pepper to gin, water to milk, sand to sugar and earth to
pepper. Additions were made to colour, to increase in
bulk or artificially to strengthen a substance:

> In 1773 a smuggler named Rushton operating in
> the Poole district was employing many people in
> the area around Wimbourne in collecting elder leaves

1   _The discoveries of J[ohn] Poulter, alias Baxter_ (6th edition,
     1753) p. 30. I am indebted to John Styles for this reference.

2   Thompson, 'Moral economy', pp. 97-8.

3   Tobias Smollett, _The Expedition of Humphrey Clinker_ (1771)
     quoted in Sir Jack C Drummond and Anne Wilbraham, _The Englishman's
     food: a history of five centuries of English diet_ (Jonathan Cape,
     1939) p. 231.

which were left to wither in barns and lofts and
then wet in water in which sheep's dung had been
steeped in order to colour them before being
dried and mixed with smuggled tea.[1]

High prices encouraged malpractices. In 1799 the rise
in salt prices saw a notable increase in adulterations of
that article and spices, tea and coffee were especially
likely to be tampered with. It was naive of the *Reading
Mercury* to observe on an outbreak of short-weighting in
butter in 1801 that although prices were enormous, 'a fair
and reasonable price will not satisfy the avaricious'.
Horrifying instances of adulteration may have increased with
the growing sophistication of food purveying. In 1788 con-
fectioners and gingerbread bakers were entreated to give up
the practice of 'frosting' their cakes with ground glass.[2]
Accum's *Treatise on the adulterations of food and culinary
poisons* (1820) called attention to the use of red lead as a
colouring in cheese and lead and copper in confectionery.
After his disgrace, public outcry was subdued until the
Lancet investigations of the 1850s which resulted in the Food
and Drugs Act of 1860. Although Engels in his *Condition of
the working-class in England in 1844* had ranted long on the
subject, his work was not translated into English until 1885.

Whether giving short weight or measure, falsely increasing either by the addition of cheaper substances or disguising
short weight by the addition of heavy articles such as coins
in butter, the unscrupulous dealer could hope to 'get away
with it' in many instances. He could escape detection entirely,
take advantage of the confusion over standards or simply rap-
idly decamp. Small men with little capital at stake might, as
Engels suggested, move to Chorlton if no longer trusted in

1   John G Rule, 'Social crime in the rural south in the eighteenth
     and early nineteenth centuries', *Southern History*, I (1979)
     145.

2   *Hampshire Chronicle*, 21 January 1799; *Reading Mercury*,
     24 August 1801; *Hampshire Chronicle*, 28 January 1788.

Ancoats.[1] One would presume that Bob the packman took care
not to visit the same haggling woman twice. The agitation of
the 1770s by resident tradesmen against the pedlar and the
packman arose not only from an understandable resentment at
the discrepancy in outlay which enabled them to undercut and
a traditional prejudice against the trade poacher but also
from the knowledge that 'The shopkeeper has a credit, a
reputation to preserve in the place where he resides, whereas, these itinerants have nothing to check an inclination for
extortion'.[2] Lumped along with the crew of thieves, the
Irish Toyles, who used itinerant trading as a front to gain
entry into houses for purposes of robbery, and tainted with
the reputation of the wanderer for the seduction of lonely
women, the outrage of the settled trader at the hawker was
understandable, even if the protection of vested interest
lay at the bottom of it.

In the otherwise exhaustive *Complete English tradesman,*
Defoe refers only to receiving and passing false money, the
use of shop rhetoric and false lighting and the breaking of
promises of payment in his chapter on 'honesty and veracity
in dealing' and the 'customary frauds of trade'.[3] A more
accurate picture emerges from the pages of Grose's *Dictionary
of the vulgar tongue:*

> rum chubb: among butchers, a customer easily
> imposed upon, as to the quality and price of
> meat ...
> Whispering Dudders: cheats who travel the
> country, pretending to sell smuggled goods
> ... The goods they have for sale are old

1   Eg 'The Court Leet Jury last Thursday took from Roger Cumner,
     shop-keeper and baker in Silver Street, 26 gallons of bread,
     being deficient in weight upwards of 140 oz and in which were
     found 3/5 worth of penny pieces', *Reading Mercury,* 22 August
     1803. Engels, *Condition of the working-class,* p. 104.

2   *Hampshire Chronicle,* 11 January 1773.

3   Daniel Defoe, *The complete English tradesman* (1745, 1841
     edition) chaps. xix and xx.

> shop-keepers, or damaged ...
> A freezing vintner: a vintner who balder-
> dashes his wine ...
> A bawdy house bottle: a very small bottle,
> short measure being among the many means used
> by keepers of those houses to gain what they
> call an honest livlihood ...[1]

The frequent 'holier than thou' announcements in the
local press that prosecutions for trading fraud tended to
fall on outsiders are denied by their own reporting of the
regular prosecutions of home-based traders. Nevertheless it
should be remembered that to the settled trader in a small
community the preservation of a good name and a reputation
for honest dealing were important: 'A tradesman's credit and
a maid's virtue ought to be generally sacred from evil
tongues'.[2] Trading was a competitive business and rumours
of malpractice were commonly used - or even created - by
rivals to injure reputations.

Several questions need to be answered still. Were the
perpetrators of fraud in trade dishonest generally in other
aspects of their lives or was their dishonesty 'compartment-
alised'? How often was prosecution simply bad luck and how
often the result of a 'last straw' in a no longer tolerable
period of dishonest trading? Many such questions cannot be
fully answered from the evidence and certainly not from the
present state of research. Nevertheless the evidence would
seem to deny overwhelmingly any picture of the eighteenth-
century market place as a settled, tranquil scene of openly
honest exchange and bartering such as was presumed of Reading
in the mid-nineteenth century:

> the business of the day, however important, and
> the commercial transactions of the week, however
> extensive, are carried on in the proper way,

1   See for example *Dictionary of the vulgar tongue* (reprint of
     the 1811 edition, Illinois: Digest Books, 1971).

2   Defoe, *Complete English tradesman*, p. 150.

> with calmness and good humour, amidst smiles and
> shaking of hands; the news of the week is blended
> with the negociations of the day, and the bargain
> is concluded with a joke.[1]

Tranquillity was not broken only in years of food riot.
Malpractice and criminal dealing were common and expected
features of eighteenth- and early nineteenth-century trading.

---

1   W Fletcher, *Reading past and present* (1841) p. 29. See also
      Cobbett's description of fairs and markets as trading centres
      where, 'the transactions are fair and just, not disfigured,
      too, by falsehood, and by those attempts at deception which
      disgrace traffickings in general' (*Rural rides* (Penguin
      edition, 1967) p. 479).

THE MILITIA MUTINIES OF 1795

Roger Wells

The first eight years of war against revolutionary
France, 1793 to 1801, were an unique experience for Britain.
The political issues generated by the French Revolution,
notably the dissemination of democratic ideology, provided
an unparalleled challenge to the British establishment. For
not only were the ruling elite, which provided those who
vied for political power, split over the fundamental issue
of parliamentary reform but the period also witnessed the
first genuinely popular working-class movement for constitutional change. The proposition split society at every
level. The decision of the younger Pitt's Tory ministry to
commit the country to what was increasingly interpreted as
a *bellum internecinum,* hardened these socio-political
divisions. While the strength of the peace movement - led
by the Foxite Whigs - fluctuated with peaks in 1795, 1797
and 1800-1, at no time was the nation united behind the war.

The war effort entailed an unprecedented mobilisation
of men and deployment of material resources. British gold
maintained her allies' armies in action on the continent.
Britain's major aggressive military role involved her navy.
Nevertheless, garrisoning the empire and providing an army
at home to guard against threatened invasion necessitated
a massive increase in the regular army and the permanent
embodiment of the Militia. The establishment of the
nation on a war footing resulted in intense competition
for men between the navy, the regular army and the Militia,
which was aggravated by the creation of an amateur army by
the Volunteer movement. Several statutory instruments
were introduced to facilitate maximum mobilisation. Naval
service was not popular; the press-gang picked off skilled
seamen from the mercantile marine and through the Quota
Acts a levy was laid for men for the Royal Navy on all

counties, inland as well as maritime. Service in the
regular army was abhorred in working-class circles; highly-
paid metropolitan artisans were 'a description of men ...
no army can ever hope to acquire', wrote an observer.[1]
Extreme poverty drove Britons into the army; regiments
raised in the West Riding were 'filled with recruits from
Sheffield, Leeds, Halifax, etc ... the very sweepings of
the streets'.[2] Others 'opted' for the army to escape the
courts.[3] War Office directives to the contrary were
negated by the competition between rival recruiting
parties.[4] Increasing reliance on crimp houses, brothels
where contrived recruitment entrapped the unwary forni-
cator, was reflected in serious rioting in London in
1794.[5] The army also depended heavily on the Irish,
whether resident at home or domiciled or itinerant in
Britain. If 'the life of a soldier was hard even by
[Irish] working-class standards ... he was at least
sumptuously dressed'.[6] Moreover the army at least
ostensibly guaranteed a full stomach; recruiting parties
patrolled the streets 'with a pig stuck on a pike and a
leg of mutton on a halberd - symbols of plenty that

1   National Library of Scotland, Melville Ms 1048, ff. 83-4, 'a
    tradesman of rather an inferior rank', London, to H Dundas,
    13 April 1798.

2   Rev. H Zouch, Wakefield, to Earl Fitzwilliam, 14 April 1792,
    cited in Ernest A Smith, *Whig principles and party politics:
    Earl Fitzwilliam and the Whig party,* (Manchester University
    Press, 1975) p. 133.

3   For examples, see Oldham Leisure Centre, Rowbottom diary entries,
    3 and 22 January 1794; *Reading Mercury,* 16 January 1797.

4   John R Western, 'Military service as a punishment', *Journal of
    the Society for Army Historical Research,* XXXII (1954) 89.

5   John Stevenson, 'The London "crimp" riots of 1794', *International
    Review of Social History,* XVI (1971) 40-58.

6   Robert B McDowell, 'The army' in Robert B McDowell, ed. *Social
    life in Ireland 1800-45* (Cork: Cultural Relations Committee
    of Ireland, 1976) pp. 73-4.

awaited the full-blown soldier'.[1]

Recruits to the regulars commonly found that their
destination was the hated West Indies. Resistance,
including desertion, to service in the Caribbean was normal.
No soldier, however ignorant, was unaware of the shocking
level of mortality from disease rather than action against
the enemy or rebellious slaves. Nevertheless there were
palliatives in the form of 'cheap rum and willing negro
and mulatto women ... to counteract the fear of yellow
fever'.[2] Enlistment in the Militia, constitutionally
ineligible for overseas service, provided an alternative.
Militiamen could expect a full stomach and a favourable
reaction from women living in the proximity of quarters
without the exposure to action and disease which was more
or less certain in the regular army. The number of militiamen rose from 30,000 in 1794 to 42,000 in 1796, when the
idea of a supplementary Militia was first mooted in the
cabinet.[3]

The Militia was concentrated on the southern and
eastern coasts - the most likely objectives of a French
invasion force. Pitt's barrack-building programme, designed
to isolate the military from exposure to the subversive
tactics adopted by some of the more militant popular democrats, was concentrated in the towns, notably in the
industrial centres in the midlands and north. Barrack
accommodation was inadequate to contain all the troops
amassed in maritime counties. A severe burden on accommodation in many locations automatically materialised. Poor

1   Thomas H McGuffie, 'Recruiting the ranks of the regular British
    army during the French wars', *Journal of the Society for Army
    Historical Research*, XXIV (1956) 54.

2   I am indebted to Dr Michael Duffy of the University of Exeter for
    allowing me to read his unpublished paper 'Motivation and
    performance in the British expeditions to the West Indies during
    the war against Revolutionary France', from whence this quotation
    comes.

3   John R Western, 'The County Fencibles and the Militia augmentation
    of 1794', *Journal of the Society for Army Historical Research*,
    XXXIV (1956) 3.

billeting arrangements were commonplace. In 1795 the
Mayor of Hastings reported

> that the great complaint among the troops, and
> ... a well grounded one, is the want of better
> accommodation in Quarters, which, under the
> present circumstances, it is impossible for us
> to give them, as the Houses are crowded with
> Soldiers - every Alehouse housing above twenty
> men billeted upon it.

One regiment which found itself in typical difficulties was
the soon-to-be notorious Oxfordshire Militia. The
accommodation available at Horsham was 'not very inviting';
a forced march of a further twelve miles to Steyning
followed but even here additional payments were required to
induce innkeepers to make 'the best accommodation for the
men which their crowded apartments would admit of'.[1]

Fraternisation with host communities commonly produced
altercations.[2] At York, off duty soldiers were denied
entry to Goodramgate pubs, whereupon they resorted to
'behaving riotously ... with drawn swords in the street'.
A constable who intervened was 'cut violently with a sword
over the face'.[3] The garrison town of Colchester was the
scene of constant disturbances. During one, members of the
Bench and a whole posse of police were assaulted by officers
who prevented the arrest of their men, an episode paralleled
at Lewes when Lord Bateman, the commanding officer of the
Herefordshire Militia, ordered the men to 'Break the ranks
and fall upon' the townsmen.[4] Troops were regularly
involved in thefts, suggesting that they took refuge in

1   Public Record Office (PRO), War Office (WO), 1/1088,ff. 133-6,
     Mayor of Hastings to the War Office, 21 April 1795, *Sussex Weekly
     Advertiser,* 26 January 1795.

2   John Western, *The English Militia in the eighteenth century*
     (Routledge & Kegan Paul, 1965) pp. 426-9.

3   PRO Assizes, 4Q/39/2/13, depositions of William Horshaw and
     Private George Elvidge, November 1796.

4   *Nottingham Journal,* 29 April 1797. *Sussex Weekly Advertiser,*
     27 April 1795, reporting a civil case between Constable Lee and
     Bateman respecting an incident eleven months earlier.

numbers and openly defied the law. One victim, a
Nottinghamshire farmer, discovered a band of soldiers
blandly driving a flock of geese out of an enclosure.[1]

The circumstances of 1795, however, were more
conducive to fraternity between the Militia and the
populace. The harvest of 1794 was substandard and prices
rose as the scale of the deficiency became increasingly
obvious as threshing progressed during the winter.[2] The
1794-5 winter was also the third hardest of the century.
The Thames froze over when temperatures rarely rose above
freezing point from late December to March; parts of the
country had to contend with very heavy snowfalls and
subsequent severe flooding.[3] In the early spring all food
prices began to accelerate. The wholesale price of a
quarter of wheat at Chichester during the first weeks of
December, February and April was 52s, 56s and 64s.[4]
Such price increases, when demand for labour was at its
seasonal lowest and working families needed to spend more
on fuel and clothing, produced a considerable fall in
living standards.

Public assistance under the Poor Law, supplemented
by hundreds of local short-term subscription charities,
guarded the most exposed sectors of the working class
against the worst effects of inflation and unemployment.
But militiamen were not protected, whether they lived in
barracks or billets. They too were victims of rapid

1   Nottinghamshire County Record Office (CRO), Quarter Sessions Roll,
     Midsummer 1799, depositions of E and J Voce, 18 May 1799.

2   *Hereford Journal*, 14 January 1795.

3   Thomas S Ashton, *Economic fluctuations in England 1700-1800*
     (Oxford: Clarendon Press, 1959) p. 25. *York Chronicle*, January
     to March 1795.

4   PRO Ministry of Agriculture and Fisheries, 10/278, 279.

inflation. The amount of bread and meat supplied was
either reduced or, in the case of the latter, maintained
at the expense of quality. The impact of price rises was
thus more pronounced on militiamen than on the workers
among whom they lived. As the Herefordshire Militia
informed Lord Richmond, the country people were relieved
by their parishes and subscriptions, the soldiers
received no such benefit.[1]

Accelerating price increases in the eighteenth
century commonly provoked protests and disturbances, many
towns being the scenes of riots in which the crowd fixed
food prices at its notion of a fair price. In some
locations popular action was extended to the interruption
of shipments of food supplies to distant markets, the
crowd insisting on retention for local consumption.[2]
While many local Benches exhibited a pronounced sympathy
with the protesters and intervened on the consumers'
behalf in disputes with retailers (the Mayor of Exeter
typically fixed commodity prices half way between those
set by the crowd and those demanded by the sellers)
disorder threatened to escalate. The south-west was the
first region to experience a conflagration, one informant
reporting from Devon that mobs were continually rising in
the market towns.[3] The onus for the restoration of order
in the absence of an effective police devolved on local
Volunteer Corps and the army, especially the Militia.
However, the latter entertained the same grievance and were
drawn from the same social ranks as members of the crowd.
Militiamen too held the same notions of a fair price and
the retention of local stocks for local use.

1   PRO WO 1/1092, ff. 139-47, Richmond to W Windham, 13 April 1795.

2   The best analysis of the complexities of food rioting is Edward P
    Thompson, 'The "moral economy" of the English crowd in the eight-
    eenth century', *Past and Present,* no. 50 (1971) 76-136.

3   Nottingham University Library, Portland dep. PWF 9847, R Eastcott
    to Lord Rolle, 28 March 1795. Cornwall CRO, Carew Mss CC/K/25,
    W Smith, St Burdeaux, to R Pole-Carew, 16 April 1795.

The Militia - and units of the regular army - were
soon to prove that they were not the willing tools of
authority when ordered against the crowd. In the south-
west, Volunteers protected market places against virtual
insurrections of Cornish miners[1] but at Plymouth and
Devonport the Northamptonshire Militia made common cause
with the townsfolk. On the morning of 2 April maximum
prices were imposed on all foodstuffs and the troops then
supervised sales until the Mayor took over. Devonport
market witnessed identical scenes, with retailers' entire
stocks being sold at reduced prices under military direction.
Here the solitary magistrate arrested a soldier allegedly
for stealing a loaf but this served only to infuriate the
highly-organised workers in the Royal Dockyard. In the
evening they led a huge crowd to demand the prisoner's
release. Clearly intimidated by the unity of the crowd and
the troops, the Bench 'requested' the army to 'overlook'
the soldier's offence. The commanding officer, Lord George
Lennox, objected on the grounds that military discipline
would be made impossible if troops transgressed the laws
with impunity but the magistracy secured temporary
tranquillity by compliance with the crowd's demand. The
disagreement between the Bench and Lennox was soon public
knowledge. Lennox's point was proved when the Militia
reassembled in Devonport market two days later to enforce
the prices set earlier. Tempers were soured by the
discovery of underweight loaves and sacks of potatoes and
the crowd was dispersed only by the personal bravery of
Lennox, who went 'into the middle of the mob ... unattended
by any person'. Although his troops obeyed his order to
return to barracks, he gave vent to his frustrations in a
tirade to the War Office.[2] Other troops in the region

1   PRO Home Office (HO) 42/34, J Tremerheere, Penzance, to Portland,
    11 and 13 March 1795. *Sherborne Mercury*, 20 April 1795.

2   PRO HO 42/34, Mayor of Plymouth to Portland, 6 April 1795. PRO WO
    1/1093, ff. 245-7, J Sabine, Lennox's secretary, to W Windham,
    5 April 1795. Devon CRO, Fortescue Lieutenancy Papers, D1262M/L7,
    W Elford to Fortescue, 4 April 1795.

involving themselves in similar disturbances included the Glamorganshire Militia at Bideford, the Exeter Fusilliers at Bideford and the 122nd Foot at Wells in Somerset.[1]

By this time the south was also experiencing disturbances. Most were trivial and resolved by magisterial dressings-down of those involved, though the Fordingbridge Bench decided to prosecute several women at the Assizes.[2] The first major intimation of events taking a potentially serious turn was given by striking shipwrights at Chatham. On Saturday 21 March the strikers led 'the lower class of people' to the market, where the butchers were singled out and meat prices reduced. The Bench anticipated recurrences on the following Saturday but excesses were contained by posses of special constables backed by the army. Paradoxically, the magistracy insisted that order could be preserved solely by the troops but claimed that they were needed only on Saturdays and that they should be removed from the town during the week, allegedly through fears of contamination by subversive elements. Sir Hugh Dalrymple, the local commanding officer, believed that these 'tumults' were of a 'very gentle and mitigated Nature' and refused to endorse the Bench's fears about the reliability of his men.[3] Meanwhile, the press gradually adopted a harder attitude. Anonymous menacing bills, actually distributed in December, were suddenly reported in March and interpreted as 'the dark and malevolent threatenings of gloomy malcontents ... the violent behaviour of a petulant multitude'. By the end of the month any sign of social

1   *Exeter Flying Post,* 9 April 1795.   PRO HO 42/34, Archdeacon Turner to Portland, with enclosed depositions, 25 April 1795.

2   *Sussex Weekly Advertiser,* 23 February 1795.   *Leicester Journal,* 13 August 1795.

3   PRO WO 1/1084, ff. 241-2; 1/1085, ff. 151-4, 175-7, Chatham Bench to the War Office and to Dalrymple, 25 and 26 March; Dalrymple to the War Office, 6 April 1795; PRO WO 5/102, f. 248, Norfolk Militia, marching orders, 26 March 1795. *Kentish Chronicle,* 3 April 1795.

insubordination 'deserved the execrations of all' and 'the
severest infliction of the penal statutes' was demanded
whenever the peace was broken.[1]

The Chatham Bench's fear of army identification with
popular grievances was more realistic than Dalrymple's
assumption that the army would simply obey its officers.
The process of identification was well illustrated by
even the feared and hated Irish regiments. The behaviour
of the 14th regiment of Foot, stationed in Berkshire, led
to a petition for their immediate removal. Sir George
Yonge was begged: 'in the name of God to remove ...
Lord Landaff's regmt. from this place, or else Murder must
be the consequence' for 'such a sett of villains' had
never entered Abingdon before. The petitioners alleged
that the troops menaced the entire community but another
informant explained that the privates 'made attempts to
spirit up the poorer Part of the Townsmen to attack the
Bakers and Butchers'. They succeeded. On 7 April the
Fair was interrupted, farmers and dealers assaulted and
meat and bread prices fixed. One local was arrested and
committed for trial but tempers were cooled by a magisterial capitulation to fixed prices. The Bench insisted
that they could control the townspeople but not even the
Volunteers dared to take on Landaff's warriors.[2]

There is ample evidence of rising military tempers in
the south during March. In Sussex, privates from the
Cheshire Militia, discovered poaching by the celebrated
philanthropist Barnard, refused to withdraw but 'in
defiance of their officers', who were present, 'beset
Mr Barnard's House, and threatened ... him, advising him

1   *Sussex Weekly Advertiser,* 9 and 16 March 1795.

2   PRO WO 1/1089, ff. 683-4; 1/1090, ff. 94-5; 40/17, Abingdon
    petition, 11 February; Mr Lovedan to C Dundas MP and to the War
    Office, both 8 April; Rev. Watts to Dundas, 8 and 13 April;
    Dundas to Windham, 8 April 1795.

... to prepare his coffin, as he would soon have occasion
for it'. The local constable took to carrying loaded
pistols to defend himself. The affair terminated after a
violent brawl in an Eastbourne inn. Such incidents were
symptomatic and indicate that not only were officers
sympathetically inclined towards their men but were either
fearful or powerless to stop them from illegal action.
Certainly, when troopers fixed prices in Canterbury on
28 March, there is no mention of their officers in any
report. Privates went to the butchers' stalls 'and having
had ... meat ... weighed ... to them, refused to pay more
than fourpence a pound for it ... the butchers being
intimidated ... suffered their meat to be taken'. The men
repeated this performance at the bakers and the magistracy
surmised that it was only a matter of time before the
soldiers were joined by the labouring poor. By 11 April,
when the next reported incident occurred, the role of the
troops in this and similar actions at Plymouth and elsewhere had been widely reported in the press. At Portsmouth
privates from the Gloucestershire Militia also had their
meat at 4d, before marching off under their officers. In
the evening, it was said, townsmen encouraged a 'few
recruits' to lead them to the Portsea Fair; prices were
again fixed and violence followed some stall-holders'
attempts to pack up early. Although the bulk of the regiment remained in their barracks, the Mayor could not trust
them to disperse the crowd and according to a hostile
witness, only 'published a manifesto to the people
conceived in such soothing terms, as ... collaterally
admits the power of the mob to be uncontrollable'.[1]

1   *Sussex Weekly Advertiser,* 16, 23 and 30 March. *Kentish Chronicle,*
     31 March, 17 and 24 April. *The Times,* 11 April. PRO HO 42/34,
     Mayors of Canterbury and Portsmouth to Portland, 31 March and
     12 April 1795.

On 13 April the Herefordshire Militia were involved
in two separate incidents. One division demonstrated in
Arundel while another joined a crowd reputedly several
thousand strong assembled at Chichester in response to
handbills calling for price reductions. The authorities,
both civil and military, resisted and arrested two militiamen and a civilian. The prisoners were hauled off to the
Dolphin Inn for examination, only to be released when the
crowd outside became violent. Thereafter the authorities
gave in: 'such riot could not be quelled otherwise than by
assurances given to the Rioters of their being, on the
Morrow, supplied with Meat and Bread at a reduced price'.[1]
At this point the situation began to look extremely
serious. Order was not only breaking down but could not
be restored because the major agent for its restoration
was a willing instigator and participant in disorder.
On 15 April Lieutenant Colonel Bishopp of the Lancaster
Light Dragoons, stationed at Brighton, sent a worried
communique to the War Office with intelligence from 'a
Clergyman who purposefully came over from Chichester'.
Significantly this emissary approached regular army
officers. He reported that 'Troops from Plymouth all
along the Coast to Chichester had been in a State of
Commotion on Account of the high price of Bread and
Provisions'. Bishopp reported unsupported information of
specific attempts to whip up the troops by 'seditious
People of the lower Class'. Whatever the truth here, and
it is more than probable that plebeian democrats had a few
words with soldiers whom they encountered in pubs, Bishopp
was sufficiently concerned to doubt the continued loyalty
of his own troops from 'the Example of these other Regiments'.[2]

1   PRO WO 1/1082, f. 87; 1/1092,ff. 139-47, Mayor of Arundel to the
    War Office, Mayor of Chichester to Richmond, Richmond to Windham,
    all 13 April 1795. *Sussex Weekly Advertiser,* 20 April. *Kentish
    Chronicle,* 24 April 1795.

2   PRO WO 1/1082,ff. 27-8, Bishopp to War Office, 15 April 1795.

One newspaper flatly denied the role of the Gloucester
Militia at Portsmouth.[1] Although he did not admit it to
his superiors, Bishopp paraded his men and asked for
grievances to be stated in an effort to forestall trouble.[2]
The Duke of Richmond took decisive action at Chichester.
The Herefordshire's commanding officer was ordered 'to
assemble a Picquet ... to send an Officers Patrole around
the Principal Streets every hour, to take up all the
Soldiers they find out of their Quarters'. On the morrow
he ordered a field day to get the regiment out of town
and to 'endeavour to make them sensible of the impropriety
of their Conduct'. He nonetheless felt constrained to
'promise ... them speedy redress'. Privately he believed
'that the safest way to preserve quiet will be to move
this Regiment immediately to some Barrack that can contain
the whole or separate them'. Whatever happened, the troops
and the people must be separated.[3]

Ironically the worst event in this chain of military-
inspired and assisted revolt involved troops living in
barracks and occurred four days later, a few miles east
along the coast at Seaford. The regiment was the
Oxfordshire Militia. Before the winter they had been on
prisoner-of-war camp duty but had moved to the unfinished
barrack at Blatchington near Seaford in January.
Conditions there were terrible; there were no beds and
the men slept in hammocks. The roofs leaked rain and snow
into their sleeping quarters. Cooking facilities were
inadequate. Discipline was rendered impossible through
the absence of a perimeter wall and the consequent

1   *Gloucester Journal*, 27 April 1795

2   PRO WO 71/170; this emerged later in the evidence of Major
    Atherstone at the Court Martial of the Oxfordshire militiamen.

3   PRO WO 1/1092,ff. 139-47, Richmond to Windham, 13 April 1795.
    Sussex Weekly Advertiser, 20 April 1795.

inability to mount a realistic guard. The entire regiment
was reported 'in a very unhealthy state' in mid-February.
It was during this period that Edward Cook, one of the
leaders of the mutiny, contracted 'a Fever in which he had
lost his hair'. Deficient rations added to the men's grievances for although they were supposed to have mutton and
beef alternately, they received mutton, which they preferred,
only once over the winter.

Matters came to a head on 14 April. Lieutenant Colonel
Langton 'perceived a general dissatisfaction among the Men'
and made enquiries. He found their meat 'very thin and indifferent and one piece not sweet'. Langton ordered it all
returned to the Seaford butcher who supplied it and next day
accompanied the two privates sent. The butcher retorted that
that was the best obtainable at 4½d per pound. Langton
arranged for meat at 5d per pound from another butcher on
16 April and explained to the men that this would mean some
stoppage from their pay. Although several companies were
satisfied with the new arrangement, others were not, particularly Captain Lloyd's. Langton was told that this company
'thought fourpence halfpenny sufficient for Beef' although
they would pay 5d for mutton; if they had to pay more 'they
should have nothing left for washing'. Langton failed to
persuade the men otherwise and dismissed the parade. Fifteen
minutes later 150 to 200 men set out towards Seaford saying
that they would go and be 'revenged on the Butchers'. Some
officers chased after them and made several arrests. They
were resisted and assaulted: 'we will have no prisoners, if
any, one and all'.[1]

1   There are two modern accounts of the mutiny, D Edwards, 'The
     soldiers' revolt', *Spokesman Pamphlets* no. 62 (Nottingham, nd)
     and A Durr, 'Riots, revolts and co-operation in Sussex 1795-1830',
     Brighton Polytechnic History Workshop, 1 (1980). Neither these
     nor that in John A Erredge, *History of Brighthelmston* (Brighton,
     1862) pp. 168-74, draw on the documentation comprising the tran-
     script of the Court Martial proceedings, PRO WO 71/170. The
     following account draws heavily on this source, PRO WO 1/1088,
     ff. 117-19, Capt Harben, of the local Volunteers, to the War

The officers capitulated by releasing their prisoners
and the men returned to the barracks. It was thought im-
prudent to increase the guard and instead the men were
allowed to remain assembled. The officers observed much
secretive planning and ordered the NCOs to sleep with the
privates to learn their intentions. However the sergeants
were not admitted to the secret. At 5.00 am on 17 April
Edward Cook (who had been shouldered and cheered the night
before) was seen going round the barrack with others, telling
the men to dress and take their muskets so that these could
not be seized while they were on parade. They said 'that
any Man who would not go out should be Scabbarded'. Although
one of the NCOs later deposed that he informed the officers
of what was going on then, the officers claimed that the
first they knew of the turnout was at 7.00 am when they 'heard
a Cry of turn out turn out' and saw 'the Men ... turning out,
with their Arms ... rushing out'. They assembled on parade,
ignored the officers' commands, 'said go they must ...
shouldered from the right and proceeded towards Seaford'.
The NCOs left in pursuit.

At 7.30 am 400 men with fixed bayonets entered Seaford.
They were met by the local JP and Volunteer commander, Thomas
Harben. His offer to buy them ten loads of wheat was cheered
and rewarded with a promise of committing no acts of violence
on any persons or buildings but the men insisted that they
would go through with their plans. The butchers were visited,
their meat taken to the churchyard and sold for 4d a pound.
A sergeant was 'taking an Account of it' when Langton arrived.
Having sold the meat, the grocers were forced to reduce the
prices of cheese, butter and 'every other article'. The men

Office, 17 April 1795, PRO HO 47/18; 50/4, ff. 273, the report
of Mr Justice Buller on the Special Commission; the clemency
pleas from civilians sentenced to death; Richmond to the Duke
of York, 21 April 1795. For accounts of the mutiny and subsequent trials, see also, Nottingham University Library, Portland
dep. PWF 5181, Sheffield to Portland, 29 July; Sussex Weekly
Advertiser, 20 April, 25 May and 1 June; The Times, 21 April 1795.

then went off to the inns to demand reduction of beer prices.
At this point several began to get drunk but Langton managed
to get a party to return, the men symbolically carrying
their meat upon the points of their bayonets.

During their time in the town the troops heard rumours
about the dispatch of flour from a tidemill in the Mill
Creek of Newhaven Harbour. Locally-ground wheat was normally
marketed in the west country as well as London but such
mercantile operations conflicted with popular conceptions of
morality which insisted on the preservation of local stocks
for local consumption. The militiamen automatically adopted
this belief and a large party went off to investigate the
mill. Unopposed, they took carts and horses from farmers
and the nearby artillery barracks. Fortunately the mill
owners were absent or their bodies 'should be stuck as full
of bayonets as [they] would hold'. The owner's house was
taken over and food and drink taken but when Private Weaver
took a watch from the valuables box he was kicked downstairs
by his mates. Mill employees were forced to load the waggons
with flour and several journeys were needed to carry the 168
sacks to Newhaven. Langton appeared on the scene once again
but none of this party would return.

While at the mill the troops learnt that the sloop *Lucy*,
loaded with flour the previous day, was still in the creek.
A detachment, 30 to 40 strong, was sent to stop it. The
vessel was boarded and the Captain told that 'they did not
mean to hurt or injure any of them, all they wanted was the
flour ... to lower the price of Provisions'. The ship was
taken by the soldiers to Newhaven quay.

The first consignment of confiscated flour sent to
Newhaven arrived by road with a triumphant yet properly-
formed guard. Drummer Warren earned himself the nickname
of the 'Horn Major' for his spirited trumpet blowing en
route. By 10.00 am over 300 soldiers had taken over Newhaven
and marched about with fixed bayonets. They were orderly and

and guards were mounted over each load of flour. The *Lucy*
was speedily unloaded, the flour put into carts and properly
warehoused. A total of 325 sacks were taken, most of which
were eventually recovered except for a very few sacks sold
'to those who chose to purchase'.

By midday most of the men were suitably installed in
the inns and too drunk, so their officers later said, to
be approached. Disorder increased. Landlords were forced
to finance the drinking by purchasing flour at reduced
prices. Some flour was exchanged directly for drink. And
the men discussed more ambitious projects. When Harben
appeared he was told 'that they were going to Demand of the
Brewers to serve the publicans with Beer at such prices that
they might afford to sell it at 4d per Pott'. When Adjutant
Frenchard ordered Cook to return, 'he postively refused told
him he had business to do, as he meant to go to the Graziers
and Farmers in the County'. These statements indicate that
the town retailers of meat and beer had placed the blame for
high prices on their suppliers and that the troops were pre-
pared to respond by forcing price reductions on the producers
but the Oxfordshire never got round to these projects.

At 1.00 pm things looked very serious with the troops
in full control of Newhaven. Parties scoured the town for
ammunition and one went to the nearby cliff-battery but
Harben had put his Volunteers in charge and the militiamen
were frustrated. The constable of Newhaven had rushed off
to Lewes where the County Sessions were sitting. The chairman, Lord Sheffield, sent immediately to the War Office and
Pitt himself discussed tactics with General Officer Commanding Ainslie. The General decided to go to Newhaven but such
was the apprehension among the magistracy at Lewes, that
only the newly-elected sheriff volunteered to accompany
Sheffield to join Ainslie. Sheffield secured the services
of the Royal Horse Artillery. They were met outside Newhaven
by Langton and agreed to try to persuade the Militia to return rather than to use force at the outset. But a party

from the Artillery accompanied Langton back to the town.
The Militia beat to arms and drew up facing the Artillery
with fixed bayonets. There was no violence but militiamen
tried to subvert the Artillery privates: 'if we [the
Dragoons] would not be for a big loaf, they should take care
of us'. However Captain Shadwell, commanding the Artillery,
managed to get the Militia to agree to a parley and negoti-
ations commenced in the comfort of the Ship Inn.

Despite the initial show of steadfastness, the arrival
of the Artillery clearly frightened the Militia, who had not
succeeded in obtaining much if any ammunition. The Militia
agreed to return with their own officers, 'but not with the
Dragoons', and obeyed Langton's order 'to Shoulder and return with him to the Barracks'. About 5.00 pm they set off
'peaceably and willingly Singing God save the King all the
way down the Street'. But as they reached the bridge at the
west end of town, they were reminded of their oaths, taken
earlier, not to re-cross until they had accomplished their
aims. A cry of 'no Bridge no Bridge' went up and sixty men
fell out of the column, determined to form a guard over their
flour for the night. Fearing that he might lose the 200 plus
who remained in the column, Langton let the minority go and
the guard remained unmolested, while Langton got the bulk of
his men back to Blatchington. Unapprised of this development,
the Artillery returned to Lewes, though Sheffield had taken
the precaution of putting the battery in a naval officer's
charge and moored a loaded ordnance vessel, which arrived
during the afternoon, under the cliff.

Before the evening, civilian participation was minimal.
At Seaford the Militia 'were encouraged by eight or nine
towns women' and Harben was forced to use 'every effort to
prevent the Country people from joining them'. The initial
reaction of the people of Newhaven is unrecorded but Shadwell
saw only militiamen covered in flour on his arrival. But
once the first episode was over and only the guard remained
in Newhaven for the night, some civilians joined the soldiers

in their inevitable drunken orgy. The soldiers used the
White Hart as their headquarters, 'took by force whatever
Liquors and other things they thought proper, and did considerable damage to ... [the] Furniture'. Private Blake felt
compelled to station himself at the top of the stairs to
protect the publican's expectant wife from molestation. The
landlord, John Inskip, later sent the Treasury a bill for
nearly £27. Damages to 'Glasses Plates Muggs ... Tables
Broke ... Windows, Doors & Locks Broke' came to £2 16s. The
bill for 'Eating' came to £2 5s, exclusive of 'Five Hams'
worth £3. The drinks bill was phenomenal, with £11 5s worth
of beer (600 pints at least), £4 6s worth of 'Shrub' and a
further £2 15s 4d worth of spirits.[1] When food at the inn
ran out, civilians, by now in the soldiers' company, directed
them to grocer Greathead, who was unpopular locally, and
showed them the grocer's cellars. These were looted and food,
clothing and other articles taken. In the melee Greathead's
watch disappeared. Eventually the troops went to bed. One
of the NCOs, who later persuaded a Court Martial that he remained in the town to try to maintain some control, organised
the billeting. When the regulars took the town the next
morning they found sleeping militiamen in beds and stables
all over the place.

About 6.30 am the following morning, Saturday 18 April,
the Royal Horse Artillery returned to Newhaven accompanied
by the Lancashire Fencibles from Brighton. Captain Harben's
Volunteers also attended. Many militiamen had only just gone
to bed and were unable to defend themselves when parties from
the Fencibles scoured the town with drawn swords and 'attacked
the Rioters wherever they could find them'. The Militia could
put up only a token resistance as they poured out onto the
streets. Colonel Bishopp was 'knocked off his horse, by a man
against whom his sword was uplifted'. Many militiamen refused

1   PRO Treasury 1/770/3196, petition of innkeeper John Inskip
     for damage, 27 June 1796.

to give up their arms. Colonel Leigh struck Private
Woodmarshall under the eye with his sword before Woodmarshall
surrendered. The militiamen were eventually all arrested
after a prolonged fight, while Harben's men mounted guard
over the flour.

The soldiers who returned to Blatchington were warned
that they would be 'cut to pieces by the Dragoons' if they
attempted to re-enter Newhaven. This served only to increase
the men's determination: 'we have begun it, and we will go
through with it'. Private Haddock 'would as soon be Shot as
used as he was'. They 'must go to Newhaven and bring home the
Guard'. The regiment assembled at the barrack; although some
were prevailed upon to return, others were not and the main
body of 160 moved off 'promiscuously mixed together' with
their arms shouldered and bayonets fixed. They were seen
descending on Newhaven as their colleagues' arrests were com-
pleted. Forewarned, the Artillery stationed cannons in support
of the Lancashires who advanced on the approaching Militia.
The mutineers plunged into a cornfield, which offered some
protection, and faced up to the cavalry. They were fired on
by the Artillery and when one ball struck a militiaman's
musket and carried away the butt end, their resistance as a
body ended and they fled, pursued by the Fencibles. Even so
some men refused to give up without a fight and an hour passed
before they were all taken. Two Fencibles were wounded, one
seriously, but several militiamen were severely wounded by the
Fencibles, many of whom broke their swords in the skirmish.

Altogether over 200 militiamen taken prisoner were
escorted back to Blatchington and their arms sent to Lewes.
Nineteen men were incarcerated in Lewes prison where they
joined the two civilians arrested for their part in the raid
on Greathead's shop. The authorities set about their prosecution and those selected for trial were transferred to
Horsham. The area remained very tense with fresh but less
serious riots being reported. Militiamen participated in
some. At Guildford and Petersfield troops led the crowd in

price fixing exercises. The Militia doing duty at Porchester
Castle 'carried their resentment and boldness' to the extent
of threatening to liberate French prisoners unless prices
were immediately reduced. Elsewhere the populace encouraged
the troops billeted among them to imitate the Oxfordshire
Militia. At Reading, one Mackall, 'a fellow of dissolute
and notorious character', was overheard by Captain Wilson
uttering seditious expressions to his men of the Sussex
Militia and a mayoral handbill suggested that he was not
alone in his endeavours. Local authorities took great alarm.
The Mayor of Hastings testified to the 'exemplary loyalty'
of the Warwickshire but after the Newhaven incident, in the
same breath asked for them to be removed as he had learned
'of the conversation which pass'd among some persons belonging
to the Corps, of their intentions to enforce the Sale of
butcher's meat next Saturday at reduc'd prices'.[1] The press
devoted enormous space to the mutiny and even at Oldham,
Weaver Rowbottom heard of the event and, unlike other home
news from afar, felt it warranted a note in his diary.[2]
Thereafter rumours of other regiments participating in riots
were vigorously and repeatedly denied by the press and disturbances in Kent at the beginning of May were not reported.
However the maximum coverage was accorded to field days and
military alacrity.[3]

Fears that the troops had been seduced into provoking
disturbances by democrats increased. Colonel Sloane, who
was to preside at the Court Martial, wanted 'to discover
whether this mutiny, and the Consequences attending it,
solely originated in the Regiment itself, or was begun, and

1   Sussex Weekly Advertiser, 20 and 27 April. Kentish Chronicle,
    24 and 28 April. The Times, 25 April. Reading Mercury,
    27 April. PRO HO 50/4,ff. 277-88, Richmond to York and reply,
    21 and 22 April. PRO WO 1/1088,ff. 133-6, E Milner jr to the
    War Office, 21 April 1795.

2   Oldham Leisure Centre, Rowbottom diary, entry 12 June 1795.

3   Kentish Chronicle, 24 April. Reading Mercury, 27 April.
    Sussex Weekly Advertiser, 20 April, 1 June and 27 July 1795.

pressed to the Extent to Which it went, by any ... persons
unconnected with the Regiment'. This enquiry was vital because 'there has been more of this spirit ... in this
District ... than in any other'. Sloane forgot that Militia
regiments were concentrated on the south coast but non-
military authorities kept a sharper look-out for potential
instigators. The Mayor of Hastings' attention was drawn to
a new resident who, it was reported by the proprietor of a
rooming house, was 'employ'd generally in reading Paine's
Rights of Man and Brothers' *Prophecies*[1] and regularly wrote
to Lord Stanhope, the radical peer, and to Mr Perry, the imprisoned editor of the Whig *Morning Chronicle*. The stranger
had also 'taken infinite pains to mix with the Soldiers whenever an opportunity has offer'd, giving them money to drink
etc'. The Mayor suspected him to be the author of a pamphlet
demanding that the Corporation fix food prices, which had recently circulated in the Borough. Although this character
decamped before the receipt of the Home Secretary's warrant
for his arrest, there is no concrete evidence of democrats'
activities and the Court Martial also failed to elicit any.
However, the expression of these fears is important. Others
showed theirs in different ways. The richer inhabitants of
Lewes and district publicly thanked the Artillery and
Fencibles and subscribed £50 for the NCOs and privates. The
inhabitants of Newhaven who had incurred most of the damage
also offered their thanks, though they failed to express this
in monetary terms. One newspaper correspondent thought that
the time for radical measures had come. The profits of landlords, bakers, butchers and millers should be made 'pro-
portional to general distress and loss'. However the proposed
meetings for voluntary profit cuts did not materialise.[2]

1 A millenarian writer who achieved national notoriety in 1795
   and was committed to Bedlam on Home Office orders. See John
   F C Harrison, *The second coming : popular millenarianism
   1780-1850* (Routledge & Kegan Paul, 1979) chapter 4.

2 *Sussex Weekly Advertiser*, 20 April. PRO WO 72/17, Sloane to
   Sir Charles Morgan, 23 April 1795. PRO HO 42/34, 52, Milner
   to Portland, 5 May 1795 and 15 October 1800.

More ominous signs appeared in the aftermath of the mutiny. At Brighton disputes arose 'between some Regiments of Militia and the Lancashire Fencibles who are called by the Militiamen, SHORT-LOAF, --BLOODY-BACK etc for their part they took in quelling the mutiny'. Moreover the unrest among other Militia regiments posed further problems. Richmond was worried about the effect of keeping so many men locked-up, a great 'Risk for they ... have all the opportunities of concerting future Plans of Mischief or Resistance'. The Oxfordshire at least should be removed immediately from their present quarters:

> for the Inhabitants of the Neighbourhood and particularly those who are ready to appear Witnesses, against them have been with me earnestly to entreat for the Removal ... as they say they are pointed out as objects of the Revenge, and that they may take it in a private way, which makes them fear for their Lives.

Presumably other militiamen and local workers also constituted a threat. In the event a bizarre incident, itself symptomatic of the prevailing apprehensions, can be seen retrospectively to have concluded this series of incidents. The Royal Horse Artillery returned to Lewes after dealing with the Oxfordshire and replaced their cannon on Spital Hill outside the town, on which a guard was mounted. About 2.00 am on 21 April one of the guard 'heard one of the guns in motion' and found it had moved forty yards. The guard panicked and a messenger was despatched to headquarters at Lewes. He arrived with 'his sword broken, not in battle, but by a fall in his haste' to allege 'that on his road he had passed a body of men, in number about 200, standing quite still near the windmill'. Bugles sounded the alarm and the Artillery assembled with the Lewes Volunteers. Rumours spread like wildfire; 'six or eight hundred men had gained possession of the Artillery's cannon and that it was the intention ... first to seize the arms taken from ... the Oxford Militia ... deposited in the old House of Correction' before releasing the prisoners. Expresses were sent to Richmond and the War Office. Regular and Volunteer regiments converged on the town later in the morning and

'the whole day exhibited a scene of military parade and
public confusion'. No confirmation of the guard's fears
was possible but none of the members changed their story
when they made formal declarations. The Lewes press concluded
that 'there remains much of this terrific mystery to be developed' and could only state that at present 'we look up to
the YEOMANRY CORPS, as the foremost to support order and good
government'. The military authorities thought otherwise; the
Duke of York's formal thanks were relayed to the regiments
which opposed the Oxfordshire and their officers made further
subscriptions for the rank and file.[1]

The government reacted very quickly. Before planning the
prosecution of the Oxfordshire, ministers decided - it seems
very largely on the prompting of Richmond - to remedy the
militiamen's major grievance. The Duke suggested that all
men should receive rations instead of cash allowances. On
14 April, the day after Richmond first wrote in connection
with the Chichester riots, Secretary-at-War Windham was informed that Pitt seemed clearly of the opinion that Richmond's
remedy should be adopted 'because the next month would be the
most likely to produce disturbances'. The order for Militia
officers to issue bread to their men was made on 18 April and
another for meat on 25 April after the Oxfordshire had clearly
demonstrated that they would not accept short rations of
animal food either. The troops were informed immediately.
Those in the south-east also received a homily from Richmond.
He trusted that the soldiers would see that while every
attempt at disorderly proceedings would be 'resisted with
vigour and punished with severity', every attention would be
'paid to their real wants, when properly and regularly represented through their officers'. When the orders were issued
the Secretary-at-War was conveniently absent from the House
of Commons. As the Foxite Courtenay later complained in the
House, the extra was

1   *Sussex Weekly Advertiser,* 27 April and 1 June 1795.

> given to the soldiers as a mere gratuitous
> donation of the King himself, and it was
> evidently intended thereby to impress on
> the minds of the soldiers that it was the
> King alone, and not the representatives of
> the people, who ... were to pay the whole.[1]

This was not merely Whig constitutional oratory. The remedy of the militiamen's grievance was coupled with the strongest appeal to the men's patriotism.

It was this rather than the harsh and much publicised retribution meted out to the Oxfordshire which won the Militias over. The Mayor of Hastings reported that the remedial measures had satisfied the Warwickshire Militia and that he no longer entertained fears of their loyalty. Later Private Cook, pleading for his life, told the Court Martial that

> great complaints were made as to the dearness
> of all kinds of provisions which has in some
> measure been since relieved by his Majesty's
> most gracious interposition with Regard to
> Bread and Meat which allowance to a Common
> Soldier is a material alteration.

The Militia were not subsequently involved in any reported disturbances, though Pitt was sufficiently displeased in the May debate on the allowances to reprimand the opposition for referring to past incidents.[2] Ministers' sensitivity over the subject led to the prosecution of newspaper editors who erroneously claimed that troops were involved in riots. Another report, of soldiers rioting at Plymouth, was ordered to be investigated by high authority.[3]

1 For the orders and the debates, see *Debrett's Parliamentary Debates*, 2nd series, XLI, 333-47. PRO WO 1/1092, f. 149, unsigned undated memo. *Kentish Chronicle*, 24 April 1795.

2 *Debrett's Parliamentary Debates*, XLI, 333-47. WO 1/1088, ff. 151-4, Mayor of Hastings to the War Office, 26 April 1795.

3 PRO Treasury Solicitor, 11/944/3431-2, prosecution briefs involving reports of disturbances at Bristol and Okehampton. PRO HO 42/34; 43/6, p. 437, Lt Col Sneyd and Portland to Lord Uxbridge, 23 May and 19 June 1795.

It is hardly possible to exaggerate the alarm felt in
government circles over the Militia mutinies; their seriousness is comparable to the Naval mutinies two years later.
Richmond was adamant that 'speedy example should be made' on
the grounds that 'the manner in which this Business is treated
may by its effects decide whether we can or cannot in future
depend upon the Militia'. To this end Richmond sought to
inflict 'some real punishment ... upon all the Men who were
taken resisting in Arms'. He admitted that as they numbered
in excess of 200 they were too numerous for 'all of them to
undergo the utmost rigor of law' but suggested government
should examine the possibility of seeking legislation to send
'them to the West Indies, or on Board the Fleet'.[1] We do not
know whether ministers took this suggestion seriously but
almost every other proposal made by Richmond was implemented.
There is no doubt that the government wanted severe measures
taken and the Commander-in-Chief was ordered to discuss
strategy with the Home Office.

In Sussex Richmond began his investigations immediately.
Three days after the effective collapse of the mutiny, he had
twenty-two men selected for prosecution. Only two of these
were to face regimental Court Martial. Fourteen were to be
tried by a General Court Martial which was able to inflict
the death penalty. Any of these who escaped punishment under
military law were to be arraigned with the remaining six
'reserved for criminal Prosecutions in the civil Courts',
with two civilians. Arrangements for the General Court
Martial were complete by 23 April. Only Militia officers
were eligible. Colonel Sloane was appointed president on the
grounds of his experience and membership of the Commons; if
necessary he could 'afterwards give an account ... of Proceedings' to MPs. Other members included Lord Rolle and Colonel
Bastard MP. The General Court Martial, which sat from 5 to
22 May, appears, from its own detailed record of proceedings,
to have been scrupulously fair. One of the fourteen was not

---

1   PRO HO 50/4,ff. 273-83, Richmond to York, 21 April 1795.

tried and four others were acquitted. Three men, all of whom
had clearly played a significant role in planning the descent
on Seaford, were sentenced to be shot. The remaining six were
sentenced to between 500 and 1500 lashes. None of those
acquitted were subsequently tried by another court and one of
those capitally sentenced was pardoned on condition of serving as a soldier in New South Wales. One of the men sentenced
to flogging received a free pardon and the sentences on the
others were reduced but not sufficiently to negate the in-
struction that only 300 lashes were to be administered at
once. The executions and floggings were scheduled for 13 June,
all but two calendar months after the mutiny.[1]

    Richmond advocated and obtained a Special Commission of
Assize to try the others on the grounds that the normal county
Assizes would not meet until August. Although this was not
announced until 15 May, it sat immediately after the General
Court Martial. Eventually four of the soldiers and the two
civilians were tried. All were charged with capital larceny;
Private Sykes and Sansom with stealing £13 and £10 worth of
flour respectively and the latter also with the theft of
6s 6d worth of rum; Privates Midwinter and Avery were jointly
charged with the theft of 1000 bushels of flour valued at
£250. The civilians, Henry Brook and John Etherington, were
jointly accused of riotous assembly and the theft of a watch
and clothes valued at £2 5s 6d from the grocer's store at
Newhaven but the jury's 'merciful intention ... to destroy
the capital part of the charge' reduced the valuation to
39s 6d. The trials of Midwinter and Avery had to be postponed to the Summer Assize because the prosecution was unable
to contact the sailors from the sloop *Lucy*. But Sansom and
Sykes were convicted and the judge was unable to afford the
prisoners 'the smallest hope of mercy in this world', ob-
serving that the case 'was attended with some very aggravated
circumstances'. Perhaps it was but Mr Justice Buller's claim

1   PRO HO 50/4, ff. 273-83; WO 1/1090, ff. 295-300, 71/170, 72/17,
     Sloane to Morgan, 23 April, Judge-Advocate to Richmond, Court
     Martial minutes. *Sussex Weekly Advertiser,* 11 May 1795.

that one circumstance was 'the AMPLE PROVISION made for
Militiamen' was ridiculous. For the extra allowance then in
force was the product of the revolt of the Militia; indeed
these men died for the cause of better provision.[1]

The executions of the men sentenced by the Special
Commission were also scheduled for 13 June. But the announce-
ment of the Court Martial sentences was greeted by incendiary
letters dropped in and around Brighton, threatening that 5000
men would appear to rescue the militiamen; these in turn provoked rumours that three regiments, 'abetted by the lower class
of inhabitants', had declared their resolution to prevent the
executions. In the event Brightonians were able to offer sympathy and to smuggle food and drink to the men sentenced to
death. Reactions to the anticipated sentences of the Special
Commission have to be gauged from the massive augmentation of
the Lewes police from the surrounding area and the failure of
'the occasion to bring together more than were necessary to
form the Grand Jury'. A particularly blood-thirsty political
doggerel circulated in the town:

> Soldiers to arms, arise your Cause
> On those bloody numskulls, Pitt and George ...
> You are sent for by express to make a speedy return
> To be shot like a crow, or hang'd in your Turn ...
> Haste soldiers now, and with intrepid Hand
> Grasp Sword and Gun to save thy Native Land
> For see your comrades murder'd, ye with Resentments
> swell
> And join the Rage, the Aristocrat to quell ...

The reality of the 'indisposition' which rendered the clergyman who delivered the Assize sermon inaudible must remain an
open question. There were some moves to obtain reprieves for
the militiamen and hopes were raised when misplaced formal
orders caused a flurry of courier activity between London and
Brighton. But in fact the authorities were planning a most

---

1   *Sussex Weekly Advertiser*, 11 and 25 May, 1 June 1795. PRO HO
     43/6, p. 395; 50/4, ff. 273-83; 51/148, f. 97, Richmond and
     Portland to York, 21 and 26 April; Portland to the Lord Chancellor,
     5 May 1795.

impressive execution ceremony and had drafted in many extra
troops, some of which had just returned from service on the
continent, to quell fears and to insure against rescue
attempts.[1]

According to the Judge-Advocate, the King regarded the
military execution of the men sentenced by the Court Martial
'indispensably necessary for the restoration and support of
discipline'. For that reason 'the execution of the Sentences'
was ordered 'to be public as may be and ... conducted with
the utmost solemnity'. The authorities intended the display
as a warning to all regiments in the country and not as a
simple retribution against the Oxfordshire. Richmond was informed that the executions and floggings were to take place
at Brighton Camp in the presence of all the Troops, Regulars,
Fencibles and Militia encamped there.

> Copies of the ... Sentences are to be circulated
> among all the Corps without exception in the
> District under your command which having been
> distinctly read to their Men assembled together,
> under arms, for that express purpose, are to be
> enter'd in their Orderly Books, to the end that
> their Comg. Officers may from them be better
> enabled, to support a Uniform Course of Regular-
> ity, a sound Discipline amongst them by holding
> up to them, if necessary, so striking an Example,
> of the fatal Consequences, that must attend their
> suffering themselves as Soldiers, to be led
> astray from their Duty, or to be governed by any
> other principals, than those of a strict obedi-
> ence to their Officers.

These instructions were sent to every regiment in the
country.[2] The seriousness of the matter can be accurately

---

1   PRO WO 81/20, ff. 93-7, 100, reprieve petitions. *Sussex Weekly
     Advertiser*, 25 May, 1 and 15 June. *The Star*, 29 May. *Gloucester
     Journal*, 8 June 1795. Erredge, *History of Brighthelmston*, p. 170.
     Douglas Hay, Peter Linebaugh, John G Rule, Edward P Thompson and
     Calvin P Winslow, *Albion's fatal tree: crime and society in
     eighteenth-century England* (Harmondsworth: Penguin, 1977)
     Appendix IV.

2   PRO WO 3/13, pp. 211-12; 3/28, p. 104; 1/1090, ff. 295-300.
     General order, Commander-in-Chief, 15 May; Adjutant-General to
     Richmond, 22 May; York to Richmond, 25 May 1795.

gauged from the ceremony. Infantry regiments lined both
sides of the site near Brighton Camp, with cavalry and
artillery troops assembled in their rear, 'a number of loaded
cannon pointed at the spot where the unhappy men suffered'.
The High Sheriff reported that 'The scene was the most awful
and impressive I ever beheld'. Nor surprisingly, 'Not the
smallest sympton of opposition, resistance, or revenge
appeared'. The floggings came first:

> The men capitally convicted were then marched
> up between the two lines of the army accompanied
> by a clergyman, and escorted by pickets from the
> different regiments of horse and foot; at the
> upper end of the line, after a short time spent
> with the clergyman, they were shot by a party of
> the Oxfordshire Militia who had been very active
> in the ... riots, but had been pardoned ... the
> awful ceremony was concluded, by the marching of
> all the regiments round the bodies ... laid upon
> the ground.

As if this was not sufficient for men who had just shot their
mates, the pall-bearers were covered in blood which had
'oozed out' of the coffins on the way to burial.

The Sheriff then proceeded to Horsham to supervise the
executions there. Although there were emotive scenes between
Sansom and his wife, who had travelled from Oxfordshire to be
with her husband, there were no reports of disturbances. Instead newspaper readers were treated to an horrific account
of the 'bungling job' performed on Sansom by two professional
hangmen who had attended from the Old Bailey, a heart-rending
mention of a subscription mounted 'by the gentlemen' to de-
fray Mrs Sansom's 'expenses ... and to comfort her under her
distress' and a brief description of the 'becoming behaviour'
of the men on the scaffold.[1]

The Home Secretary's relief at 'the good order and behaviour of the troop's at Brighton' might be inferred from

---

1   *Sussex Weekly Advertiser*, 15 June. *Reading Mercury*, 15 and
     22 June 1795. Erredge, *History of Brighthelmston*, p. 174.

his report to the King, who had devoted some time to fully
mastering 'the question of the sentence of death by a Court
Martial'. The Sheriff of Sussex piously hoped that 'An example so unusual and so terrible will ... have the desired
effect'. But the obvious satisfaction of authority did not
extend to reprieving both the other two soldiers sentenced
to death at the Sussex Summer Assize. Avery, who was 'half
a fool' according to the judge, was reprieved. The Grand
Jury considered 'the example already made' on 13 June
sufficient and asked for Midwinter's reprieve. The trial
judge saw no reason to comply and the Home Secretary placed
the burden of a decision whether the examples already made
had 'satisfied ... the Justice of the County' on to Lord
Sheffield. His Lordship thought that the reprieve of Avery
'under pretence of his having a weak understanding' sufficient
for the purpose of a display of mercy. Sheffield had 'heard
of no circumstance in favour of Midwinter' and concluded 'that
if better discipline is not established in the Militia they
will become the curse of the Country. As the Officers are
not apt to enforce it I cannot recommend relaxation in such a
case to the Civil Power'. This 'candid opinion' sealed
Midwinter's fate.[1]

1   *Reading Mercury*, 22 June 1795. Portland to George III and
     reply, both 14 June 1795, in Arthur Aspinall, ed. *The later
     correspondence of George III* (5 vols, Cambridge University
     Press, 1962-70) II, 305-6. PRO HO 48/5, trial judge to
     Portland, nd. Nottingham University Library, Portland dep.
     PWV 109, ff. 154-6; PWF 5181, Portland to Sheffield and reply,
     28 and 29 July 1795.

FROM CUSTOM TO CRIME: WOOD-GATHERING IN EIGHTEENTH- AND
EARLY NINETEENTH-CENTURY ENGLAND: A FOCUS FOR CONFLICT
IN HAMPSHIRE, WILTSHIRE AND THE SOUTH

Robert W Bushaway

A chapter of John Evelyn's great work *Sylva, or a
discourse on forest trees and the propagation and
improvement of timber in his Majesties dominions,*
entitled 'Of the laws and statutes for the preservation
and improvement of Woods', contains the following
sanguinary statement:

> Severer punishments have lately been ordained
> against our wood-stealers, destroyers of young
> trees and etc. By an ancient law of some Nations
> I read he forfeited a hand, who beheaded a tree
> without permission of the owner; and I cannot say
> they are sharp ones, when I compare the severity
> of our laws against mare stealers; nor am I by
> inclination the least cruel but I do affirm, we
> might as well live without Mares, as without
> Masts and ships, which are our wooden, but no
> less profitable horses.[1]

Laws against wood-stealers never quite invoked the
harsh retribution advocated by Evelyn. However, the
eighteenth century saw the progressive strengthening of
sanctions in a way which would have, in part, satisfied
the celebrated diarist as English landowners protected
the source of England's 'wooden horses' from wood-
stealers and destroyers of young trees.

Wood-stealing has not attracted the student of
eighteenth-century social history in the same way as more

---

1   John Evelyn, *Sylva: or a discourse on forest-trees and the
     propagation of timber in His Majesty's dominions* (1870 ed.)
     p. 206.

dramatic infringements of the law.[1] The armed affrays
between poachers and game-keepers which frequently occurred
in the copses and covets of the English countryside are
reasonably well chronicled, although much more remains
to be done in terms of motivation, protest and the
relationship of the crime to the community. We now also
know of the bitter conflict which took place between
small farmers and royal officials in the Royal Forests
of Hampshire and Surrey and which took the form of
bands of disguised men poaching deer.[2] In some areas
smuggling was tolerated and promoted by the local
inhabitants to such a degree that the authority of
government exisemen was openly and defiantly challenged
to the extent that, for some of the time, these areas
were beyond the force of the king's law.[3] For example,
in March 1795 a 'posse comitatus' was raised in Hampshire
to protect and escort to the Winchester Assize some
witnesses who were to give evidence against a smuggler.
The first attempt to escort the witnesses to Winchester
ended in failure as the party was forced back to
Southampton by a large body of smugglers, all armed and
mounted.[4]

The dramatic nature of the tensions and conflicts
aroused by these forms of crime explains their attraction
to social historians concerned to dispel the myth of the

1   See the relevant studies in Douglas Hay, Peter Linebaugh,
     John G Rule, Edward P Thompson and Calvin Winslow, *Albion's
     fatal tree: crime and society in eighteenth-century England*
     (Harmondsworth: Penguin Books, 1977) and James S Cockburn, ed.
     Crime in England 1550 to 1800 (Methuen, 1977).

2   Edward P Thompson, *Whigs and hunters: the origins of the Black
     Act* (Harmondsworth: Penguin Books, 1977)

3   Calvin P Winslow, 'Sussex smugglers' in *Albion's fatal tree*,
     pp. 119-66.

4   *The Annual Hampshire Repository*, I (1799-1800) 9.

tranquillity of eighteenth-century English society. As well as being dramatic, such crime was aggressive, self-assured, confident and often violent. The punishments for such violations of the Palladian peace of mind were severe. Transportation, hanging or periods of imprisonment awaited the convicted poacher, deer-stealer or smuggler.

In fact possibly the most common way in which the law and rights of landed property were infringed was by the taking of wood from parks, woodlands, copses and hedgerows. A brief survey of summary conviction records for Wiltshire indicates that wood theft or damage was a consistent and frequent occurrence. Furthermore, the difficulties involved in detection and prosecution of wood-theft - unless caught red-handed or convicted on the evidence of witnesses, it was hard to prove guilt - make it seem probable that the number of crimes reported from which convictions resulted represents only a very small proportion of the number committed and that illegal wood-gathering was widespread.

Poaching, smuggling and deer-stealing were always acknowledged as infringements of the law, despite popular sympathy and encouragement for them. Indeed, in the case of deer-stealing, the criminal became folk hero and entered mythology. However, Robin Hood retained his potency because he stole from the rich and gave to the poor, rather than because he opposed oppressive forest laws. It is the nature of Robin Hood himself which makes the crime acceptable. The eighteenth century witnessed the application of harsher penalties and perhaps a greater increase in the commission of such crimes as poaching and smuggling.[1]

1 See Eric J Hobsbawm, *Bandits* (Harmondsworth: Penguin Books, 1972) pp. 41-56 and John G Rule, 'Social crime in the rural south in the eighteenth and early nineteenth centuries', *Southern History* I, (1979) 141.

The taking of dead wood was anciently a popular
right, protected by customary law and sometimes recorded
in manorial charters. Wood-gathering occupied a central
position in the popular view of relationships within the
community, similar in importance to such practices as
gleaning - the claim to harvest perquisites - harvest
homes and largess and to other annual ceremonial claims.
Possibly, the protection of public rights of way across
private land (usually enclosed) can also be placed in this
category as it involved disputes about access to commons.
The transition from custom to crime occurred in the late
seventeenth and eighteenth centuries as the wood-gatherer
faced increased legal sanctions and was more regularly
stigmatised as a wood-stealer.

'Through all the woodland parts of this county',
wrote Charles Vancouver in his 1808 account of agriculture in Hampshire:

> the peasantry are tolerably well supplied
> with fuel, and which is obtained by a claim
> they exercise pretty freely, of taking what
> is called 'snapwood'; that is all the fallen
> branches, and such as they can snap off by
> hand, or break down with a hook fixed in the
> end of a long pole; for this purpose they
> have been observed to visit most of the
> demesnes and private as well as other wood-
> lands through the county.[1]

The custom of taking snapwood existed also in
Wiltshire where the specific rights of tenants to wood
can be seen in an early seventeenth-century charter
relating to the inhabitants of Great Wishford. This .
charter, known as 'The sum of the Ancient Customs

---

1   Quoted in William Marshall, *A review and complete abstract of
     the reports to the Board of Agriculture from the Southern and
     Peninsular Departments of England* (York, 1817) p.317.

belonging to Wishford and Barford out of the Forest of
Grovely', sets out the precise nature of the customary
rights belonging to the inhabitants of Great Wishford
with respect to wood gathering in nearby Grovely Forest.
In fact the charter specifies a whole series of common
rights such as pannage and grazing for cattle. The
rights are extensive:

> Item the lordes and freeholders of Wishford
> and Barford for themselves and all theire tennants
> and all inhabitants in the said mannor of
> Wishford and Barford St Martyn have an auntient
> custome and ever tyme out of minde have used
> to fetch and of right may fetch and bring away
> Bowes at theire pleasure from the woodes of
> Groveley from Maye daie in the morninge untill
> Whit-Monday at night every Saterdaye and half
> Hollydaie once vizt in the eveninge and every
> hollydaie and Sabbath daie twice vizt in the
> morninge and in the Eveninge.

> Item the lordes and freeholders of Wishford
> for themselves and theire Tennants have ever
> by auntient custome and tyme out of mind used
> to fell in Groveley and in right may lawfullie
> fell and bring away aboute Holie Thursday
> everie yeare one loade of trees uppon a Cart
> to be drawen by strenght of people and the lord
> and freeholders of Barford for themselves and
> thier tennants have used and in right may
> fetch one other loade of Trees uppon Whitson
> Munday uppon a Carte to be drawen also by
> strength of peopell.

> Item the old custome is and time out of mind
> hath byn that the people and Inhabitance of
> Wishford and Barford aforesaide may lawfully
> geather and bring away all kinde of deade
> snappinge woode Boughes and Stickes that be in
> the woodes at Grovley at their pleasure without
> controlment and none other besides them may
> lawfully fetch any there at any tyme.

In order to reaffirm these rights, each year it was laid
down that

> the lords freeholders Tennants and Inhabitance
> of the Mannor of greate Wishford or soe many
> of them as would in auntient tyme have used to
> goe in a daunce to the Cathedrall Church of our
> blessed Ladie in the Cittie of newe Sarum on

Whit Tuesdaie in the said Countie of Wiltes,
and theire made theire clayme to theire
custome in the Forrest of Grovely in theis
words: Groveley Groveley and all Groveley. [1]

Other ceremonies associated with wood gathering
can be identified. In Huntingdonshire the following
custom was observed:

It is the custom at Warboys for certain of
the poor of the parish to be allowed to go
into Warboys Wood on May-day morning for the
purpose of gathering and taking away bundles
of sticks. It may possibly be a relic of the
old custom of going to a wood in the early
morning of May-day for the purpose of gathering May-dew. [2]

On 5 November at Charlton on Otmoor, children sang:

The fifth of November, since I can remember,
Was Guy Faux, Guy, poke him in the eye,
Shove him up the chimney-pot, and there let him die.
A stick and a stake, for King George's sake,
If you don't give me one, I'll take two,
The better for me, and the worse for you.
Ricket-a-racket your hedges shall go. [3]

Yet another custom connected with wood gathering prevailed at St Briavels in Gloucestershire:

On Whit Monday several baskets full of bread
and cheese, cut into small squares of about
an inch each, are brought into the church,
and immediately after Divine Service is ended
the churchwardens, or some other persons, take
them into the galleries, from whence their
contents are thrown among the congregation
who have a grand scramble for it in the body
of the church, and the tumult on these occasions
is always very great; sometimes, indeed, of a
character very ill suited to a sacred edifice.
The custom is held for the purpose of preserving

1   Printed in Rev. Edward H Steele, *The history of Oak Apple Day
    in Wishford Magna* (Salisbury, 1951) pp. 9-13.

2   *Notes and Queries*, 3rd series, XII (July-December 1867) 42.

3   *Oxfordshire Archaeological Society Reports for 1903*, p. 31.

to the poor of St Briavels and Hemelfield   sic.
Hewelsfield the right of cutting and carrying
away wood from three thousand acres of coppice
land in Hudknolls and the Meinds, and for which
every housekeeper is assessed 2d, to buy the
bread and cheese given away.[1]

The assessment of 2d per household is probably a survival
of 'wood coin' - a payment formerly made by tenants of
some manors to the lord for the right of gathering dead
wood.

The Great Wishford charter shows the familiar
manorial customs of Plowbote, Hedgebote, Housebote and
Firebote. These customs were reserved for the tenants
and inhabitants of Great Wishford and Barford St Martin.
Indeed, the charter further contains a number of
presentments for infringement of these rights by outsiders:

we present that the Inhabitants of Barwicke
St James, Stapleford, Stoford, Newton,
Chilhampton, Ditchampton and Wilton do often
use as namelie goodwife White of Stapleford
and others there, John Hoop of Stoford and
divers others there, John Baker of Everall
the Clark of Newton and divers others there,
and out of Ditchampton some and out of Wilton
very many doe often resort into Groveley
woodes and fetche fearne and wood there without any auethoritie for the doeinge thereof.[2]

Of the forms of wood custom, firebote seems to
have been the one which survived longest and was most
jealously guarded. As specified in the charter, at
Great Wishford the right to 'snappinge wood' was
open to all people and inhabitants of the village.

1   *Berrow's Worcester Journal*, 2 June 1836. The custom
    is still observed.

2   Steele, *Oak Apple Day*, p. 15.

This right assumed a significance in the popular mind
for two reasons. Firstly, fuel was a most important
commodity and one which was expensive. Secondly, the
right to gather dead wood in areas where this was
plentiful helped shape a view of the relationships
within the community between the poorer inhabitants
and their richer neighbours in which the factors of
unity and corporate identity were central.

The taking of green wood, on certain days and for
certain periods in the year, by tenants for building
purposes was a right which was also common in customary
relationships. May-Day figured importantly as one of
the days when the taking of green wood was legitimate.
I believe it is for this reason that May-Day is
associated, even today, with so great a variety of
ceremonial practices which are connected with wood and
wood use. The Maypole itself is no more than a tree
taken from the woods and set up on the village green.
John Evelyn points to this when he wrote:

> And here we cannot but perstringe those
> Riotous Assemblies of idle people, who
> under pretence of going a maying (as they
> term it) do oftentimes cut down, and carry
> away fine straight trees, to set up before
> some Ale-house, or revelling-place, where
> they keep their drunken Bacchanalias.
> I think it were better to be quite
> abolished amongst us, for many reasons,
> besides that of occasioning so much wast
> and spoil as we find is done to trees at
> that season, under this wanton pretence by
> breaking, mangling, and tearing down of
> branches, and entire arms of trees, to
> adorn their wooden idols.[1]

For example, the notion that the tree was usually
stolen can be seen in the following: 'What adoe make
our young men at the time of May? Do they not use

[1]   Evelyn, *Sylva*, pp. 206-7.

"night watchings" to rob and steale young trees out of other mens grounde and bringe them home into their parishe with minstrels playing before'.[1] It is clear that this practice persisted into the seventeenth and eighteenth centuries:

> The most of these May-poles are stolen, yet they give out that the poles are given them – There were two may-poles set up in my parish *[King's Norton]*; the one was stolen and the other was given by a profest papist. That which was stollen was said to bee given, when 'twas proved to their faces that 'twas stollen, and they were made to acknowledge their offence. This pole that was stollen was rated at five shillings: if all the poles one with another were so rated, which were stollen this May, what a considerable sum would it amount to.[2]

Indeed the custom of taking a growing tree for May-Day survived into the late-nineteenth century in Herefordshire at Letton and at Upper Chilstone, Madley.[3]

29 May or Oak Apple Day (the anniversary of the restoration of Charles II) was another occasion for the ritual taking of wood; 'As much injury is generally done to oak trees on 29th May, we think it right to mention that three persons of Botley, Hampshire, were lately sent to prison for six months, for cutting boughs from oak trees in that parish'.[4] Oak Apple Day was also the day of the Great Wishford ceremony.

1   *Treatise against dicing* (1577) quoted in John Brand, *Observations on popular antiquities chiefly illustrating the origin of our vulgar customs, ceremonies and super-stitions* (2 vols, London, 1813) I, 194.

2   Thomas Hall, *Funebriae florae, the downfall of May games* (1660) quoted in Brand, *Popular antiquities,* I, 200.

3   Ella M Leather, *The folk-lore of Herefordshire* (Sidgwick & Jackson, 1912) p.18; *Transactions of the Woolhope Naturalists Field Club,* 1924, p.82.

4   *Berrow's Worcester Journal,* 27 May 1819. I am indebted to Mr Len Smith for this reference.

Custom was an essential feature of pre-industrial society. As John Stuart Mill wrote: 'The farther we look back into history, the more we see all transactions and engagements under the influence of fixed customs'. 'Custom', he continued,

> is the most powerful protector of the weak
> against the strong; their sole protector
> where there are no laws or governments
> adequate to the purpose. Custom is a
> barrier which, even in the oppressed
> condition of mankind, tyranny is forced
> in some degree to respect . . . But
> though the law of the strongest decides,
> it is not the interest nor in general
> the practice of the strongest to strain
> the law to the utmost, and any relaxation
> of it has a tendency to become a custom,
> and every custom to become a right. Rights
> . . . determine . . . the share of the
> produce enjoyed by those who produce it.[1]

It is against the background of custom that we should view what can only be described as a battle which took place in the eighteenth and early nineteenth century between landowners and wood gatherers. The belief that there existed a customary right to collect deadwood for fuel, which included the taking of wood from growing trees 'by hook or by crook' or by 'snapping' as well as from the ground, prevailed in the popular mind. In order to gain a proper impression of what was implied by the act of gathering wood, the historian must lay aside the image of the poor man gathering sticks in the King Wenceslas carol. Wood gathering involved the taking of all forms of wood where such wood could be gathered either from the ground or from the branches with only the effort of snapping it off or by using a crooked pole. The use

---

1   John Stuart Mill, *Principles of political economy* (Toronto University Press edition, 1965) p. 240.

of any other tools such as saws or billhooks was not
legitimate with regard to growing timber. These were
systematic and regular methods of obtaining fuel and
should not be viewed as sporadic or casual. However,
the distinction between green and dead wood had grown
up in manorial custom regarding firebote and was clearly
open to much dispute. Overzealous gleaning of the
branches of a growing tree obviously brought down
much live wood as well as dead and in practice the
distinction was hard to define. The pattern of legal
sanctions in the eighteenth century was to prohibit
even the smallest infringement of the rights of
property in wood in order to prevent widespread
ravages and despoiling. It is probable that this was a
reaction against generous interpretations of 'snapping
wood' in the seventeenth century.

Yet the right to gather wood occupied as important
a place as corn gleaning in the popular mind and in
the economy of the labouring poor and was based on the
customary rights of manorial tenants and local
inhabitants to snapping-wood. Furthermore, in the
face of increasing hostility from landlords, some
tenants continued to practice their presumed right to
take greenwood, although this was less common. I am
similarly convinced that many harvest perquisites can
be found to have their origins, however distant and
transformed, in the labour services and customs of
manorial practice.

There were two crucial periods of legislation
relating to offences concerning wood. The first occurred
in the early years of the Restoration. During the
seventeenth century enclosures, particularly in wooded
areas, provoked several sustained, determined and
organised disturbances. In the 1630s, in the south and
west, particularly in Dorset and Wiltshire, opposition

to enclosure of forests was strong. Disturbances
occurred at Braydon in Wiltshire and Feckenham in
Worcestershire in 1632, and in 1634 in Gillingham in
Dorset. A figure, dressed in woman's clothes and
referred to as 'Lady Skimmington', led a determined
band in the destruction of enclosures in the Forest of
Braydon, near Purton in Wiltshire. Three of the ring-
leaders were eventually arrested, each fined £500 and
ordered: 'to be set in the Pillory in women's clothes
as they were disguised in the Riots, with papers on
their heads declaring their offences and be there well
whipped'.[1] This serves as a remarkable reminder of the
potency of the symbolic dressing in women's clothes
during popular disturbances and in this case illustrates
how the authorities attempted to defuse the symbolism
by turning it back on the rioters in the form of
ridicule.

Rioters in women's clothes and wood-gatherers
might not, at first, appear to be associated, but as
well as being concerned with the immediate target of
the enclosure fences themselves, the rioters were
concerned to establish the general right of access to
the woodlands and to secure for the local community
benefits of pannage, grazing for cattle and the
gathering of wood for fuel.

In the Civil War it is probable that forest and
woods were further exposed to visitations of wood-
gatherers, 'without controlment', to use the phrase

1   *Calendar of State Papers Domestic 1631-33*, pp. 67, 74;
     Records of Star Chamber Cases Trinity II Charles I 1633,
     Public Record Office Sta. Cha. 9: 'A case of riotous
     destroying of inclosures in the forest of Braydon'.

employed in the Great Wishford charter, so that by the Restoration it was necessary to extend statute law in that area. A statute in 1663, the legal change to which John Evelyn referred, gave power and authority to apprehend 'all and every person or persons they shall suspect, having or carrying, or any ways conveying, any burthen or bundles of wood, underwood, poles or young trees, or bark or bast of trees, or any gates, stiles, posts, pales, rails, or hedgewood, broom or furze'.[1] The statute covered a wide variety of wood forms and points at the strong anti-enclosure elements involved in the commiting of wood offences. Hedges and fences in themselves were ready sources of wood for fuel and constant despoiling could lead to them being rendered ineffective as barriers. On the other hand, they were also deliberately thrown down to gain access to woodlands and then removed as wood for fuel. This motive can be found in the following extract from the Parliamentary enquiry of 1845:

> I had some sheep in the neighbourhood
> of Luton, just by the town, and I
> frequently missed stakes, pulled up of
> a night and hurdles pulled up, and the
> sheep were let out over the fresh turnips;
> the consequence was, that one evening my
> shepherd went and took a person that had
> taken a hurdle and broken it up. I went
> down and found the hurdle underneath a
> heap of stubble. The man was found
> guilty? Yes; the punishment was about
> 6s or 7s, and he had a fortnight to pay
> it in; . . . Was the charge against the
> man before the magistrates a charge of
> stealing? - It was for stealing; it was
> not for letting out the sheep, but for
> taking a hurdle out of the field, and
> breaking it up for firewood. Was it

.1   15 Charles II c 2: 'An Act for the punishment of unlawful
     cutting or stealing or spoiling of wood and underwood and
     destroyers of young trees'.

malicious damage that you complained of,
or felony? I did not consider it felony;
it was taking the hurdle, and breaking
it up for firewood.[1]

A certain amount of ambivalence surrounded the
taking of wood from fences and hedges. The law
generally acknowledged that the crime was one of theft,
supporting the view that the wood was stolen for fuel
rather than as an act of malicious damage. This can
be seen in the trial for theft at the Easter Sessions
in Winchester in 1784 when William and Thomas Smith
were charged that on 6 February 1784 they 'feloniously
stole ten pales of wood value 10d property of the Earl
of Portsmouth'. They had been detected in making up
two bundles of pales from the fencing round Portsmouth
Park from where a great many pales had been carried
away that winter. Found guilty, they received
sentences of one week's imprisonment and a public
whipping. No attempt was made to magnify their
offence so that a charge could have been brought under
the infamously severe Black Act.[2]

The legislation gave powers of search to
constables and other officers. They could search,
on suspicion only, any property thought to conceal
stolen wood. If the accused could not give a good
account before a magistrate of how he came by the wood
or produce evidence of purchase, he was 'deemed and
adjudged as convicted' of the offence of the cutting
and spoiling of the woods, underwood, poles or young
trees concerned. The penalty for the first offence

1   *Report from the Select Committee on the Game Laws*, BPP, 1845,
     Cmd. 463, IX, pt.I, Qs. 448-54.

2   Hampshire Record Office, Minutes of proceedings of the
     Quarter Sessions QMP/2, Easter 1794, f.226.

was fixed at a maximum fine of 10 shillings with the offender being made liable for any damages. Failure to pay the fine resulted in the offender being sent to the House of Correction for up to one month or being whipped. The second offence carried the penalty of one month's imprisonment with hard labour. Buying stolen wood was also made an offence. The statute's significance lies in the comprehensive and thorough treatment of takers of all types of wood. This can only be viewed as a departure from the specification of rights to wood in manorial custom. A further statute in the reign of Charles II separated malicious damage to timber trees from the lesser offence of wood-stealing.[1]

The second significant strengthening of the law occurred in 1766.[2] The reaction of local communities in Wiltshire has indicated to Martin Ingram that wood gathering was regarded as 'an equivocal area of behaviour'.[3] The strengthening of the law in 1766 aimed to remove all possible equivocation and to establish firmly the criminality of wood gathering. It was made an offence to 'wilfully cut or break down, bark, burn, pluck up, lop, top, crop, or otherwise deface, damage, spoil or destroy or carry away any Timber tree'. The punishment for a first offence upon conviction before a magistrate on the evidence of one witness, was a fine of £20 or six to twelve months imprisonment. A second offence was punishable by an

1   15 Charles II c 2.

2   6 George III c 48: 'An act for the better preservation of timber trees and of woods and underwoods, and for the further preservation of roots, shrubs and plants'.

3   Martin J Ingram, 'Law and disorder in early seventeenth-century Wiltshire' in Cockburn, ed. *Crime in England*, p. 128.

increased fine and longer period of imprisonment. However, a third offence could bring transportation for seven years. Within the meaning of the Act, timber trees were oak, beech, chestnut, walnut, ash, elm, cedar, fir, asp, lime, sycamore and birch,[1] to which were later added poplar, alder, larch, maple and horn beam.[2] The offence of taking wood from other than timber trees, that is, underwood, hedgewood, hollies and thorns, was punishable by a fine of forty shillings or one month's hard labour and a whipping.[3] In accordance with eighteenth-century practice, detection was to be encouraged by the offer of rewards to informers. Anyone attempting to aid an offender to resist arrest was liable to a heavy fine. A further statute added that, if the offence was committed by night, an offender could be transported for seven years as the crime was then treated as a felony.[4]

Under the statute, an offender was brought before a magistrate and if, upon the evidence of one witness, he was convicted, the details of his crime and the degree of his penalty were recorded in the form of a paper slip in a standard form of words:

> Be it remembered that on the ___ day of ___ in the year ___, A B was upon the complaint of C D convicted before _____ for _____ in pursuance with an act . . .

This was duly signed, sealed and dated and then certified and filed amongst the records of the next sessions. Unfortunately such summary conviction records

1   6 George III c 48.

2   13 George III c 33.

3   9 George III c 41.

4   6 George III c 36.

rarely survive. Wiltshire, however, has a full series
and I hope to able, in the future, to make a fuller
analysis of them.

Except in cases where the crime was committed by
night or where it was a third offence, summary conviction
records, where they survive, are the only 'official'
source. In the case of night or third offences,
quarter session records prove more useful, although
the full details of the cases are not often recorded.
A major source for detailed case studies is the local
press, which for Hampshire and Wiltshire (and also
Berkshire) is rich and rewarding. It was the more
dramatic cases which were reported but this serves to
highlight the key areas involved. Advertisements
offering rewards for information leading to the
conviction of wood-stealers or notices warning possible
illegal gatherers of wood are also frequently to be
found. So the historian can expect only to glimpse
the tensions and conflicts which often ran deep in
eighteenth-century woodland society in Hampshire and
Wiltshire. Yet even these glimpses, tantalizingly
brief though they may be, give witness to powerful,
assured and determined resistance in some areas to
legal sanctions against the right to gather wood for
fuel, which was so deeply fixed in the popular mind.

In October 1787 an anxious and doubtless law-
abiding correspondent of the *Hampshire County Magazine*
gave the following warning to his fellow readers:

> You cannot render your Magazine more useful
> at this season than by giving a place for the
> following extract from the act of the 6th of
> his present Majesty, of the law relative to
> woods, as many people under the pretence of
> going a nutting may subject themselves to
> great punishment, without being fully apprised
> of the risque they run. The Act recites that

> many idle and disorderly persons have
> made a practice of going into woods,
> underwoods and wood-grounds, and cutting
> and carrying away great quantities of
> young wood of various kinds for making
> poles, walking-sticks and for other
> uses; and under pretence of getting
> fire-wood, have cut down, boughed,
> split off or otherwise damaged or destroyed
> the growth of said woods and underwoods
> to the great injury of the lawful
> owners.[1]

This letter indicates the importance the correspondent attached to warning the inhabitants of Hampshire of the risks they perhaps unknowingly ran as a result of the strengthened legislation when exercising long-established customary rights to go nutting or to collect firewood.

Further warning of a different kind appeared in the pages of the *Hampshire Chronicle* on 13 August 1792:

> Whereas the Timber growing on the estates
> in the Parish of Eling, which belong
> to Winchester College, have been cut,
> lopped and stolen by certain iniquitous
> and daring plunderers of property who are
> supposed to live in the neighbourhood
> of Bartley: A reward of Twenty Guineas
> is hereby promised to anyone who will
> give such information as may convict any
> person or persons so injurying the estates
> aforesaid.

The advertisement continued further and indicates another and obviously connected crime:

> And whereas many encroachments have from
> time to time been made on the waste of
> the College Manor, to the great prejudice
> of the College tenants, notice is hereby
> given that in future, neither the College
> nor homage of the manor, will consent

1 *Hampshire County Magazine*, I, no. xxii (October 1787).

that coppices should be granted for such
encroachments; but all buildings hereafter erected on the waste by trespass
shall be pulled down, and all land taken
in from the waste by trespass shall be
laid open. [1]

Winchester College had several estates in Hampshire,
in particular the manor of Eling, on the edge of the
New Forest and on the west bank of Southampton Water.
This manor was well-wooded and from the Wood Account
Books it can be seen that the sale of timber was a
valuable and regular source of income for the College.
It would also seem that at this time the College
decided to better develop and maintain its wooded
estates.

It became apparent that a major problem had
developed [2] in Eling with respect to wood stealing
and encroachment. In many ways these were twin issues.
Some inhabitants of Eling lived a marginal existence
on the edge of the woods, putting up buildings, taking
waste land into rough cultivation or for grazing and
gathering wood for fuel. Also, the tenants of the
College benefitted from the proximity of supplies of
wood for fuel and timber for building purposes.
In December 1794 the Wood Minute Book recorded that
great injury had been done to the woods at Eling,
particularly at Birchwood and Polsom Bushes. It
resolved that a stipend usually paid the warden and
Wood-Burser be discontinued in order that a proper
salary might be allowed out of the same for the better

1   *Hampshire Chronicle*, 13 August 1792.

2   Winchester College Muniments (WCM), f.6667.

management of these woods.[1]   The number of trees
carried away and injured amounted perhaps to some
1200,[2]   although another estimate put it much higher:
'upon a moderate calculation there have been near
3000 trees belonging to the College cut down, lopt,
and otherwise injured within the last six or seven
years'.[3]

Such despoiling demanded action and the College
was not slow in this respect. In 1792, two men gave
information on behalf and at the expense of the College
against some wood stealers at Eling.[4]   In 1793 a
thorough enquiry into the condition of the woods in
the Manor of Eling was mounted by the College. The
finding was that although the land was much suited to
the growth of good timber, it was ravaged by wood
stealers:

> Fletchwood is peculiarly adapted to the
> growth of oak timber. It has however been
> much injured by wood stealers. The cottagers
> in the neighbourhood of Fletchwood do great
> injury to the wood, and it is their common
> practice to cut down trees from the frittern
> to trees of 20 or 30 feet timber.

The report added that, 'This wood is however less
liable to Depredation than others'. 'Warden's Thorns',
the report continued:

> has likewise been much injured, tho' a
> small wood. Trees have there been cut
> and carried away, that have contained
> 30 feet and upwards of timber . . .
> Halfpenny Hern has suffered in like
> manner. Paulsham Bushes, a wood more
> adapted to the growth of Beech than
> other timber, (tho' favourable to the

1   Winchester College Minute Book, f.33, 3 December 1794.

2   WCM, f.6667.

3   *Annual Hampshire Repository*, I (1799-1800) 98.

4   WCM, Bursars account books 1787-99.

growth of oak) has been extremely abused.
It is a fact, that great part of the
timber now standing in this wood has
either been lopped, or otherwise injured.
In many parts, trees have been cut or
sawed off in the middle, and frequently
near the stool; or where the trunk remains
the most considerable lengths have been cut
away.

This report detailed other abuses: 'The Ash
timber on the Manor has been much injured by the
keepers in the New Forest, who lop them for browsing
their deer'. It also indicates why the Minute Book
recorded the stipend usually paid to the warden was
to be set aside to pay a woodward who would protect
the interests of Winchester College in the Manor of
Eling:

The extent of the college woods in Eling,
and their situation in the New Forest,
making them liable to great Depredations;
it becomes necessary to employ some active
man in that department only. The care of
the woods and the labour necessary in
keeping up the fences, will fully employ
one man; and should be his only concern.
A salary adequate to 9s a week would be
sufficient wages, and the Society would
be amply compensated by the preservation
of its timber. It does not appear that
a plan of this kind has yet been adopted by
the College. Sir Charles Mill employs a
man constantly at the above salary.

The report concluded in a rather fatalistic way that,
'Notwithstanding all possible care, the Society must
expect that these woods will be liable to considerable
depredations'.[1]

The depredations in the woods of Eling do not
appear to have been carried out by poor and landless

1   WCM, f.6667.

men. On the contrary it would seem that Winchester
College faced such damage from some of their tenants.
The problem of encroachment on wastes suggests that
squatters were attracted to forest areas to live marginal
existences on their limits. However, an earlier
document for 1760 in the College records shows that
encroachment was in fact undertaken by a good many of
their tenants.[1]

In fact, 'all possible care' was taken to protect
their woodlands. In January 1793 one John Whicker was
'convicted of cutting and lopping beach timber, the
property of the warden and fellows of Winchester College'
and was imprisoned for a year.[2] A far more sustained
effort was mounted later in the decade when it can be
said that the College achieved something of a break-
through in its battle with the 'iniquitous and daring
plunderers' of their property. There were two major
trials of Eling wood stealers in this period.

The first occurred in 1798 at the Easter Sessions.
On the prosecution of the warden and scholars of
Winchester College, William Gould, Edward Gould, Thomas
Wolfe and Stephen Hatch were charged with 'cutting down
and taking away in the night of the 28th February last,
a beech timber tree, at a place called Balsome Bushes,
in the parish of Eling, belonging to the warden and
scholars of Winchester College, lords of the manor of
Eling'. During the trial no specific mention of the use
of tools was made and it is probable that the accused
used none as it is certain that, to ensure conviction,
the prosecution would have referred to tools if they
had been used. Therefore, it is more likely that the

1   WCM, 6291 a-c.

2   *Hampshire Chronicle*, 21 January 1793.

men were merely gleaning the trees for fuel.
('Balsome Bushes' I believe to be the 'Paulsham Bushes'
of the College's report.) The woodward, Richard Light,
gave evidence of the amount of damage in the last six
to seven years, stating that in that time, 'near 3000
trees' had been injured. The principal evidence came
from William Hatch, who was one of the accomplices and
was related to Stephen Hatch, one of the accused. He
had 'voluntarily come forward as a witness' and 'swore
to the prisoners cutting down the timber and putting
the same into a cart which he had procured in order to
carry it away'. It appears that the woodward detected
Hatch and Wolfe in the act of driving the cart away
with the timber in it. As the offence was committed
by night, the full force of the law was invoked and the
prisoners were all sentenced to be transported for
seven years. A study of the lease records of the
College suggests that these men were not squatters or
poor labourers but were tenants of the College in so
far as the names can be positively identified.

At the Midsummer Sessions in 1798 a further case
was tried, against one Peter Gray. Gray was indicted
for lopping two beech trees standing on Balsome Beeches
on the night of 3 May (an interesting date bearing in
mind the variety of May ceremonies and customs
associated with wood and the citing of May in the
Great Wishford Charter as in some instances one of the
permitted periods for legal wood taking). Gray was a
previous offender, having been convicted in 1795 for
the lopping of a beech tree belonging to the College
and, failing to pay the £10 fine, he was committed to
gaol for six months. Furthermore, he had been a
witness at the last Sessions, called to give characters
for the prisoners who had been convicted and transported.
John Steed, who had given evidence against the prisoners
at the last session, 'swore to his having seen Gray

cut a large limb from a beech tree, belonging to the
College . . . it being moonlight which the prisoner
carried home with him'. Steed further stated that
previous to that in the night, 'he saw and heard the
prisoner bark and cut down a great many young trees of
different kinds'. Again, it is noteworthy that no
specific mention was made of the use of tools and it
is probable that Gray used none.

An alibi was attempted on Gray's part. Two or
three witnesses - including his sister and her husband -
were called to prove that he was elsewhere at the time
when he was charged with having committed the offence.
However, in a close examination of them their story
differed greatly from what they had said before Mr
Poulter, the magistrate who had committed the prisoner,
and the court overruled the plea: 'the whole of the
evidence having been summed up to the jury in a very
satisfactory manner by the chairman of the Court, the
jury gave a verdict of guilty'. Gray was sentenced to
transportation for seven years.

There is some suspicion in all this that Gray
was deliberately 'set up' because he gave evidence at
the first trial. If we accept that this was not the
case, then it was probably of considerable relief to
the College to rid themselves of one more desperate
wood-stealer from Eling. It would seem again probable,
although no positive identification in the leases can
be made, that Gray was a tenant of the College. The
name certainly occurs and reoccurs in the eighteenth-
century records for that manor.[1]

---

1   *Annual Hampshire Repository*, I (1799-1800) 98.

This somewhat lengthy reconstruction of the
details of the conflict which occurred in the late
eighteenth century between Winchester College and some
of the inhabitants of its Manor at Eling represents
one of those glimpses which can be made of the tensions
which wood rights aroused. It is perhaps likely that,
after a lax period in the management of its affairs,
the College sought to develop the valuable timber
resources of its estates - not an unusual entrepreneurial
decision at this time - and consequently hardened its
attitude to the taking of wood. In 1825 William Cobbett
recommended the growing of timber as a reliable and
speedy means of making profit: 'The inducements to
create property by tree-planting are so many and so
powerful, that, to the greater part of those who possess
the means, little, I hope, need be said to urge them to
the employing of those means. Occasions enough will
offer for showing how quickly the profits come'.[1]
It appears that the College faced resistance not merely
from a few individuals but from a woodland community
who depended upon the benefits of access to wood for
their marginal economies. Some of the features of
this communal solidarity can be seen in the details
of the trial: first, Gray's evidence as to the
characters of the accused in the first trial, then the
attempt to establish an alibi at his own trial.
Moreover, it was only with the aid of an informer
related to the group that evidence was found for the
trial of the two Goulds, Hatch and Wolfe. I do not
think we are talking of idle and disreputable criminals
but of men living in a community with close proximity
to woods and forest who believed that taking wood on a

1   William Cobbett, *The woodlands or a treatise on the preparing
     ground for planting, on the planting . . . of forest trees
     and underwoods* (London, 1825) Preface, item 5.

regular basis from the College estate was not a crime
but was a custom, at least defended by common practice.
No more than three months after the first trial Gray
was detected taking wood, by night, in the same area.

In the early nineteenth century the manor was
enclosed and certain specific fuel rights to turf were
set aside for tenants of the College.[1] The sharp
lessons of 1798 were not enough for the inhabitants of
Eling and further trouble seems to have occurred during
the early part of the nineteenth century. Indeed, one
writer saw wood-stealing as the first step on the road
to other forms of rural crime:

> The poor of Eling derive considerable
> advantage from the vicinity of the New
> Forest. A cottage and garden are
> obtainable at a moderate rent from
> £2 10s to £5.   Pigs are easily kept.
> Fuel, whether of turf or wood, is
> cheap, and the climate is such that
> a day's work is rarely lost through
> inclemency of weather. On the other
> hand, the Forest tempts the poor to
> become poachers and timber-stealers,
> and these nightly depredations lead to
> the robbing of out-houses of poultry and
> calves, and sometimes to house-breaking,
> and to dissolute habits of every
> description.[2]

Earlier in the eighteenth century a similar
pattern of events, although of a less dramatic nature,
can be seen in another part of the county. In this
case, the cause of the access to the woodland was
championed by legal test. At the Assizes at Winchester
in March 1776 a case was heard against one Jevoise
Clark of Belmount. Clark was accused by Peter

1   WCM, 6671. An act was passed in 1810 for the enclosure
     of the manors of Eling and Fawley.

2   Appendix of statistical information on the parish of
     Eling attached to Thomas Easton, *Statements relative to
     the pauperisation of Kirriemuir, giving an account of
     Eling and other parishes in Hampshire* (Forfar, 1825).

Taylor Esq of Pembroke Park (MP for Portsmouth) of
breaking down his park pales. Clark justified his
action by claiming a right of way across Taylor's
parkland to Purbrook Heath and also a right of common
in a close which, though formerly enclosed, had lain
open for several years past. The land in dispute was
of little value: 'never worth a shilling an acre,
being morassy and barren, part a rabbit warren, and
the remainder a peat moor'.

Several ancient witnesses were summoned to testify
to these claims ('upwards of four score years of age')
and they testified that no road had formerly lain
across the lands 'until the fences being entirely
neglected and broken down, people and carriages went
over it at their pleasure'. The report in the *Hampshire
Chronicle* continued 'All the evidences brought on the
Defendent's side were of modern date, and mostly persons
in some degree interested in the decision, as wanting
a road from Havant to Purbrook Heath', and added that
'to the surprise of most of the spectators a verdict
was found, in part, for the Defendent, Mr Clark'.

The effects of this decision were also reported:

> We are informed from Havant, Bedhampton
> and the villages adjacent, that the inhabitants
> of those places met (after the case between
> Peter Taylor and Jevoise Clark, Esqs was
> decided . . .), and spent an evening shewing
> the most evident proofs of joy, by ringing
> of bells firing of guns, and every
> demonstrative gladness that could be shewn,
> at having regained a right which was attempted
> to be wrested from them.1

1   *Hampshire Chronicle*, 18 March 1776.

This popular expression of joy did not sweeten
Mr Taylor. In September 1776, the following warning
appeared:

Wood stealers

Whereas several idle and disorderly persons
have, under a pretence of nutting or gathering
dead wood, made a practice of going into and
damaging the woods and coppices of Peter
Taylor, Esq of Purbrook Park, in this county;
now this is to give notice, that any person
who shall hereafter be found in the woods and
coppices of Peter Taylor Esq or within his
Manors of Farlington and Drayton, trespassing
against the Statute . . . in such case made
and provided, shall be prosecuted as the law
directs. And any person giving information
to Mr James Newland, in Havant, shall
receive a reward of Two guineas, on conviction
of the offender, over and above the moiety of
the forfeiture allowed by the statute.

This advertisement was again carried by the *Hampshire
Chronicle* on 7 October 1776.[1]

An interruption in the campaign occurred the
following year with the death of Peter Taylor. His
heirs, however, took up the cause, for in April 1778
one William Langley, of Plant Farm in the Parish of
Southwick, was convicted at Fareham before Richard
Bangus 'for having in his possession a quantity of
thorn bushes cut on Red-hill Plain, in the forest of
Bere, the property of the heirs of the late Peter
Taylor Esq'.[2]

Some similarities with the conflict between
Winchester College and the inhabitants of Eling, and
this struggle can be identified. Firstly, in both

1   *Hampshire Chronicle*, 30 September, 7 October 1776.

2   *Hampshire Chronicle*, 27 April 1778.

cases it would appear that control of the woodland
was lax or had been allowed to slacken over a period
of years. After the act of 1766 and in response to the
increasing attractions of efficient cultivation of
timber, the landowner sought to reassert his control
over the woodland areas in dispute. Secondly, the
conflicts occurred on manors close to Royal Forests –
Eling near the New Forest and, in the second case, in
the villages and hamlets around the Forest of Bere.
A third case, which will be referred to in more detail
later, that of the Forest of Alice Holt on the Hampshire/
Surrey border, can also be added to this list. Thirdly,
the pattern of advertisements warning potential offenders
and offering rewards leading to the successful
prosecution of wood-stealers and cases brought to trial
as reminders of the potency of legal sanction against
taking of wood is common to both cases. In the case
of the dispute in Southwick and Farlington over Peter
Taylor's woods, the remarkable feature of a benevolent
member of the gentry taking up the cause of wood rights
and right of common at court can be added. Rarely did
the poor wood gatherer find such a champion.

The crime of taking wood seems to have been widespread in Hampshire in this period. It was reported in
June 1773 that 'many people have been committed this
week to the Common Bridewell for making it their daily
practice to tear hedges; a practice very frequent and
prejudicial to farmers'.[1] A similar situation was
apparent in the 1770s in Berkshire where the same
pattern of the publishing of notices and reporting of
offences occurs in the *Reading Mercury*.

[1] *Hampshire Chronicle*, 14 June 1773.

The practices of wood-stealers in the forest of
Alice Holt were so daring and assertive that their
reputations were used in a political context.
Supporters of one side at a political meeting
advertised in 1790 were given criminal associations
as it was said that 'The county is flattered with the
expectation of a most respectable attendance of wood
stealers and poachers from the Holt Forest . . . at
the meeting on the 14th'.[1]   This reputation for wood-
stealing was founded on some dramatic occurrences.
Gilbert White of Selborne wrote:

> A very large fall of timber, consisting
> of about one thousand oaks, has been cut
> this spring (viz, 1784) in the Holt forest;
> one-fifth of which, it is said, belongs
> to the grantee, Lord Stawel. He lays claim
> also to the lop and top: but the poor of the
> parishes of Binsted and Frinsham, Bently and
> Kingsley, assert that it belongs to them;
> and, assembling in a riotious manner, have
> actually taken it all away. One man, who
> keeps a team, has carried home, for his
> share, forty stacks of wood. Forty-five
> of these people his Lordship has served
> with actions. [2]

Lord Stawall complained to the Treasury in December
1783 that the people of Frensham, 'under a pretended
right, took away not only the stack wood but also the
whole of the tops of the trees of the preceeding fall'. [3]

Of the actions against the offenders, the *Sixth
Report of the Land Revenue Commissioners* states that
in all 'upwards of Forty Actions against the poor

1   *Hampshire Chronicle*, 11 January 1790.

2   Gilbert White, *The natural history of Selbourne* (Everyman
     edition, 1912) p. 27.

3   'Sixth Report of the Land Revenue Commissioners', Appendix
     no. 17, *Journals of the House of Commons*, XLV (1790) 126.

people of the adjoining parishes, for taking away Parts
of Wood; and that they all entered appearances, but
suffered judgement to go by default'. It further records
that the same case of right to wood was tried in 1741
and found against the inhabitants of Frensham. [1]
As to the quantity of wood taken, the *Report* records
that 'the Offal Wood, after having been made into
Faggots, and a Day appointed for the Sale of it, was
openly carried off by the People of Frensham, to the
Number of 6,365 Faggots, in One Day and Night'. [2]

The same strength of unity in the community
detectable amongst the inhabitants can be seen at Frensham.
The Surveyor General's Deputy was absent there when 'the
County people began carrying away the wood' and when
he returned it was almost all gone. He detected two
men loading a waggon with part of it and got a
warrant for apprehending them; but the Tything man of
Frensham, where the offenders lived, never executed it,
though repeatedly pressed to do so and offered
assistance by the Deputy. When he applied to the
keepers and enquired whose teams had been employed
in taking away the wood, they told him they knew
nothing of it and he could get no information from them
against the offenders. [3]

The claim to take offal wood after a general fall
of timber had long been maintained in the Frensham area,
despite a judgement against the right in 1741. The
inhabitants did not step over the line into casual

1   'Sixth Report of the Land Revenue Commissioners', 126

2   'Sixth Report of the Land Revenue Commissioners', 126,
    Appendix 18.

3   'Sixth Report of the Land Revenue Commissioners', 126
    Appendix 19.

taking of wood after specific timber felling. The
Report makes this clear: 'no attempt is ever made
to take Offal wood of Trees felled by Lord Stawell's
order, and that hardly a Faggot is ever missing'.[1]
This claim was a generally held right amongst rural
labourers and forest dwellers. However, by the
early nineteenth century it had been largely
extinguished. Thomas Smart was questioned on this
point by the Select Committee enquiring into the rate
of agricultural wages in 1824. The following exchange
indicates a major shift in attitude away from custom:

> Do you cut down much timber? I do sometimes.
> Upon these occasions, you have a right
> always to as large a faggot as you can carry
> home? - No; they will not allow us any now.[2]
> Then you have it in pay, do not you? - No.

The action of the inhabitants of Frensham in
1783 was a late dramatic assertion of certain long-
held customary rights to wood. By 1824 legal opinion
and the practice of landowners had moved a long way
from the defence or even the acknowledgement of such
rights.

Against a concerted effort in parts of Hampshire
to preserve these rights in the latter half of the
eighteenth century, the altered opinion prevailed.
Philip Loveland, James Coleson, Richard Binfield

---

1   'Sixth Report of the Land Revenue Commissioners', p. 126,
    Appendix 19.

2   *Report from the Select Committee on the Rate of Agricultural
    Wages*, BPP, 1824, Cmd. 392, vi, p. 456. Smart had been
    employed at Eversholt, Bedfordshire for 20 years; he was
    married with 13 children. He received no additional wages
    during the harvest except his food. Apparently the
    tradition of paying extra wages was not observed in
    Bedfordshire although the 'bavin', a faggot tied with two
    bands, was still allowed to hedgecutters in Northamptonshire
    (Anne E Baker, *Glossary of Northamptonshire words and phrases*
    (2 vols, London, 1854) p. 36).

and Thomas Quinall were sent to Winchester Assizes
for stealing a large quantity of oak-timber from Holt
forest, 'the property of his Majesty'; whilst in
1790, 'This week was committed to our gaol, William
Wooldridge for lopping, defacing and spoiling some
oak timber, in the Holt forest'.[1]   By the 1820s
summary prosecutions were frequent but trivial compared
with the dramatic conflicts of forest communities
previously.[2]

The bitterness which remained at the steady
denial of this right can, however, be seen in a tale
recorded in the mid-nineteenth century in Wiltshire.
In a short note on stocks, the antiquary F A Carrington
recorded of the stocks at Ogbourne St George that

> about 1780 Mrs Charlotte Mills recollected
> a woman named Mary Smith being charged by
> Capt. Rudman of the Woodlands (Mildenhall)
> with taking wood from his hedge - a man
> named Hollick swore against her that she
> took the wood from a hedge in what is now
> one of Mrs Bannings meadows. She was taken
> to Swindon and brought back almost frozen
> with cold - her clothes were taken off at
> Peck Cottage and she was whipped at these
> stocks.

Mrs Mills related this account to Carrington in 1852,
some seventy years after the event, yet the bitter
memory of it still remained in the community. The
Rudman family had also been active in convicting

---

1   *Hampshire Chronicle*, 2 June, 4 August 1794. No bills were
     found which might suggest that the custom was still strong.
     Hampshire Chronicle, 22 March 1790.

2   See the account of wood stealing at Greens Norton in
     1790 in Jeanette M Hay (née Neeson), 'Common right
     and enclosure: Northamptonshire 1720-1800',
     unpublished PhD thesis, University of Warwick, 1977.

wood-stealers from Bishopstone in Wiltshire during the
1740s.[1]

Some inhabitants of Wiltshire retained the
belief that wood could be gathered by right for
fuel and that only a nominal punishment could be
inflicted. In 1806 at the Hilary Sessions in Salisbury
one John Aust was indicted 'for cropping and spoiling
timber trees in the night time' and was thereby liable
for transportation for seven years. However, the
prosecution begged for a lenient sentence as they
wished merely to 'undeceive the lower order of people'
who fancied that for such offences only a small fine
could be inflicted. Aust was imprisoned for six
months. The warning does not seem to have been
entirely heeded for in 1812 one John Gay was transported for seven years for cutting down and destroying
a maiden oak tree.[2]

The taking of wood was a long and persistent
custom throughout the eighteenth and early nineteenth
centuries among Hampshire woodland communities and the
poor in general in other areas. It was rooted in the
context of late medieval and early modern manorial
custom, sometimes crystallized in written charter
and thereby recorded. As legal sanctions steadily
changed to accommodate new attitudes to property and
to the relationship between landowners and tenants or
local inhabitants and also new attitudes to the
cultivation and management of timber plantations, so

1   Devizes Museum, Mss Notebooks of F A Carrington, 39,
    f. 89; see summary conviction records for wood theft
    in Wiltshire County Record Office.

2   William Dowding, *Fisherton Gaol: statistics of crime
    from 1801 to 1850* (Salisbury, 1855) Hilary Sessions
    entry 1806 and 1812.

this customary claim came under attack and, despite
several rearguard actions, was extinguished.

I would like to end on three notes. The first is
a poetic comment, the second represents a small but
significant triumph and the third is a microcosm of
the whole issue.

John Clare was aware that the change in attitude
towards gatherers of wood was part of an overall
transition from the ordering of relationships in
what might be called customary society (that is,
where there was a balance between the claims and
rights of the lesser members of the community and the
duties and responsibilities of the leading members in
a reciprocal relationship) to a new form of social
order, in which the importance was placed upon contract,
the cash nexus and where responsiveness to market
forces played the major role. In this transition, the
denial of the right to take wood for fuel was really
the last vestige of these claims and rights. In his
poem 'The parish: a satire' he wrote of the 'last
refuge - which is now denied' of the poor in gathering
fuel:

> Born with the changes time and chance doth bring,
> A shadow reigns, yclept a woodland king,
> Enthroned mid thorns and briers, a clownish wight,
> My Lord's chief woodman in his title's height.
> The bugbear devil of the boys is he,
> Who once for swine picked acorns 'neath the tree,
> Who gleaned their scraps of fuel from the wood;
> When parish charity was vainly tried
> 'Twas their last refuge - which is now denied.
> Small hurt was done by such intrusions there,
> Claiming the rotten as their harmless share,
> Which might be thought in reason's candid eye
> As sent by providence for such supply;
> But Turks imperial of the woodland bough
> Forbid their trespass in such trifles now,
> Threatening the dithering wretch that hence proceeds

With jail and whipping for his shameless deeds,
Well pleased to bid their feeblest hopes decay,
Driving them empty from the woods away,
Cheating scant comfort of its pilfered blaze,
That doubtless warmed him in his beggar days.
Thus knaves in office love to show their power
And unoffending helplessness devour,
Sure on the weak to give their fury vent
Where there's no strength injustice to resent;
As dogs let loose on harmless flocks at night,
Such feel no mercy where they fear no bite. 1

The small triumph was achieved at Great Wishford,
St Briavels and probably elsewhere. Wishford preserved
its rights to gather wood by continuing to practise
the annual ceremony of dancing to Salisbury and
affirming their rights in the shout before the altar
of 'Grovely, Grovely and all Grovely'. By trans-
ferring the ceremony to the more officially approved
Oak Apple Day, 29 May, the rights were preserved,
albeit in a truncated form. There were times when
the Lords of the Manor, the Pembrokes, nearly succeeded
in extinguishing the rights but in 1894 the Oak Apple
Club was founded to protect and promote them. Even
today the inhabitants gather fuel all the year round
and on Oak Apple Day process around the village
carrying a banner, very much like a Trade Union banner,
proudly proclaiming, 'Grovely, Grovely, Grovely and all
Grovely - Unity is Strength'. 2

1   John Clare, *Selected poems,* ed. John W Tibble and Anne Tibble
    (Dent 1965) p. 166.

2   The shout raised by the villagers in Salisbury Cathedral
    and during the pre-dawn perambulation of Great Wishford
    prior to the visit to Grovely Forest as well as the Club
    banner give 'Grovely' three times, although the charter
    specifies only two. This may have resulted from
    combining the Great Wishford cry with that of Barford
    St Martin where three shouts of 'Grovely' were specified.
    (See Robert W Bushaway, 'Grovely, Grovely, Grovely and all
    Grovely: custom, crime and conflict in the English
    woodland', *History Today,* XXXI (May 1981) 37-43).

And finally the microcosm. The following case was decided late in the nineteenth century at the Beaminster Petty Sessions. George Rowe and John Lane, labourers of Thorncombe, the former a married man, were summoned for stealing some pieces of timber valued at 1s 6d on 8 February 1881 at Thorncombe, the property of Captain Bragge, who retired from the Bench during the hearing of the case. PC Pike stated that on the day in question he had seen the two defendants with a cross-cut saw sawing a tree which had been blown down and was lying in a field belonging to Captain Bragge. They cut off two pieces, one of which he produced:

the chairman: 'Do you know what they were going to do with it?'

PC Pike: 'Burn it, sir, I believe; they said so.'

the chairman: 'Because if they were going to use it for any other purpose it would make the case more serious.'

Rowe admitted the offence and said he had acted through want. He had four small children and had been working all the winter for 10s a week on which the whole family had to live. Both defendants pleaded guilty and were each fined 10s including costs, 14 days being allowed for payment.[1]

---

[1] *Bridport News*, 11 March 1881. Rowe and Lane had used a saw which made their conviction inevitable. However the tree had blown down and was evidently not growing timber. Such acts of Providence were regarded by villagers as customary windfalls, in a similar manner to the popular view of wreck on the coasts. Notions of 'property' were not attached to fallen timber - the flotsam and jetsam of the countryside. The law sought to define all wood as property.

THE MANIFOLD CAUSES OF RURAL CRIME:

SHEEP-STEALING IN ENGLAND, c 1740-1840

John G Rule

> Then I'll ride all around in another man's ground
> And I'll take a fat sheep for my own
> Oh I'll end his life by the aid of my knife
> And then I will carry him home.
>
> (Dorset folksong)

To William Cobbett, poverty was the self-evident cause of increasing rural crime in the years following the ending of the great French Wars:

> the tax gatherer presses the landlord; the landlord the farmer; and the farmer the labourer. Here it falls at last; and this class is made so miserable, that a felon's life is better than that of a labourer. Does there want any other cause to produce crimes?

He sneered at those who kept 'bothering our brains about education and morality . . . who is to expect morality in a half-starved man? . . . what education, what moral precepts, can quiet the gnawings and ragings of hunger?[1]

Historians of that bleak period of English rural history which lies between the high-profit years of the French Wars and the middle of the nineteenth century have tended to follow Cobbett in linking desperate poverty among farm labourers with an increasing incidence of criminal committals in the rural counties.

1   William Cobbett, *Rural rides* (Everyman edition, 1957) I, 297-8.

The Hammonds pronounced the labourer's lot 'wretched and squalid in the extreme' and suggested that it was only through crime that he survived at all:

> He was driven to the wages of crime. The
> history of the agricultural labourer in this
> generation is written in the code of the Game
> Laws, the growing brutality of the Criminal
> Law, and the pre-occupation of the rich with
> the efficacy of punishment.[1]

More recently Professors Hobsbawm and Rudé have described the farm labourer in the years leading up to the risings of 1830 as not just pauperised but demoralised and degraded, becoming not 'merely a full proletarian, but an underemployed, pauperised one'. Especially so far as the southern and eastern counties are concerned, it is a verdict which is not easily disputed even by those with an ideological predisposition to do so.[2]

Like the Hammonds, Hobsbawm and Rudé emphasise the connection between this poverty and increasing crime in the rural counties:

> He could seek a relief from poverty in crime –
> in the simple theft of potatoes or turnips
> which constituted the bulk of the offences
> which he would himself regard as criminal,
> and in poaching or smuggling which he would
> not. It was, of course, not a mere source
> of income, but also a primitive assertion
> of social justice and rebellion.

Crime in the agricultural areas, they conclude, was 'almost entirely economic – a defence against hunger'.[3]

1   John L and Barbara Hammond, *The village labourer* (Guild Books, 1948) pp. 183-4.

2   Eric J Hobsbawm and George Rudé, *Captain Swing* (Harmondsworth: Penguin Books, 1973) p. xxii.

3   Hobsbawm and Rudé, *Captain Swing*, pp. 50, 54.

For the eighteenth century Professor Beattie's study
of Sussex and Surrey indictments tends towards a
similar conclusion. He finds a 'strong suggestion'
that property crime in the countryside was to a
considerable extent a matter of hunger and necessity
and varied in incidence with the price of food. [1]

Given the nature of the crimes which fill the
assize and sessions calendars of the rural counties
and accepting the serious level of poverty among farm
labourers, either for a prolonged period as in the
early nineteenth century or in years of harvest failure
in the eighteenth, the linking of poverty and crime
should perhaps seem as obvious to the social historian
as it did to Cobbett. Indeed poverty must be assumed
the underlying condition but is it sufficient
explanation of why rural felonies should increase in
one period or year over others? Some contemporaries
were sensitive to the complexity of the issue and
stressed a variety of causes. Sir Thomas Baring of
Hampshire who was regarded as something of an authority
on rural crime gave a list of reasons for its increase
to a select committee in 1828:

> The increase in population
> Increase of wealth of one class of the
>   population and poverty among the other
> Temptation caused by the exposure of property
>   and its transit from place to place
> The number of ale-houses and fairs
> Want of control over lodging houses
> The game laws
> Transportation sometimes inducing rather
>   than deterring crime
> Too good treatment of prisoners in the hulks
> The state of the poor laws, the bastardy laws
>   and those relating to lewd women

1   John M Beattie, 'The pattern of crime in England, 1660-
    1800', *Past and Present*, no. 62 (1974) 92.

The state of the customs and excise laws
Payment of legal clerks by fees rather
    than salary
Frequent and unnecessary commitment of
    petty offenders by magistrates, such as
    husbandry servants for disobedience of
    their masters' orders or for not performing
    their work
Want of a uniform prison system
The Act for paying prosecutors and witnesses
    their expenses which had had a short term
    effect in increasing indictments 1

Without entering into a discussion of all of
Baring's points, it is clear that he was well aware
that the level of indictments could be determined
by things other than 'real' movements in crime.
Administrative changes (fees and expenses), multiplying
of offences by laws (game laws and excise), defects in
the methods of punishment, changing temptations and
opportunities and changing attitudes to what was
considered serious enough to merit instituting
proceedings all exerted influence on the level of indictments and cannot be presumed constant over time without
investigation.

Even if poverty was a fact and accepting that
rural felonies were increasing, several possible
explanations exist. Crimes could have been committed by
rural labourers not so much as a direct result of their
poverty but rather as an expression of resentment
against that condition. Felonies might increase not
simply because poverty was extreme and widespread but
because it coincided with a decline in social order, a

1   *Report of the Select Committee on Criminal Commitments, BPP,*
    1828, Cmd. 545, vi, Minutes of evidence, p. 21.

decrease in morality, a loosening of traditional
sanctions and restraints which had previously operated
more effectively in keeping even hungry men from crime.
Increasing indictments in rural courts may not have been
at all the result of the actions of hungry labourers but
accounted for by 'invading' townspeople (much poaching
was of this kind) or vagrant groups like tinkers, beggars
or gypsies. There is at least the possibility that a
large proportion of rural crimes may have been perpetrated
by a 'professional core' of country villains who lived
by crime in the same way as many urban thieves did. This
was at least the impression which Edwin Chadwick strove
so hard to give in his loaded report of 1839 urging the
desperate need for the establishment of a rural constabulary.[1]

In case-studying an individual crime like sheep-
stealing we should reasonably expect to find instances
which fit all of these categories. The problem is one
of weighting the various motivations. Sheep-stealing
offers good possibilities for investigation. As mutton
is food then hunger motivation is possible but since
sheep are also a moveable and transferable form of property so too are 'professional' motivations. As a
capital felony, cases would finally come before the
assize courts and not be 'lost' to the historian in the
areas of lower courts and summary jurisdiction. It was
too a sufficiently common crime to have generated a good
deal of documentation and being covered by specific act
is extractable from the statistical series. In this
paper I have cast a wide net over regions and sources
although with a distinct bias to the western counties

1   See Samuel E Finer, *The life and times of Sir Edwin Chadwick*
    (Methuen, 1952) pp. 167-74.

where most of my research was done. The wide cast was
deliberate. It seemed necessary to get an idea of
attitudes and assumptions on the matter of sheep-stealing
rather than a detailed count of incidence in one selected
area. Than can still be done; doubtless one of the new
generation of historians of crime is already hard at
work doing it now.

'I back toe thee kitchen, feelinge verrie sorrie
for thee poore retches if they hav done thee steelinge,
for itt be a serious thyinge toe steele a sheepe',
wrote a Herefordshire farmer's wife in her diary in 1796
when she heard two men had been taken for stealing a
neighbour's sheep. It was indeed a serious thing.
Under an act of 1741 it was a capital felony without
benefit of clergy - a hanging matter. The act had
followed the petitioning by farmers and graziers from
Essex and Middlesex complaining of increasing night-
time depredations on their flocks. A committee was
appointed to hear the evidence of the petitioners and
within ten weeks from receipt of their petition the
farmers got their wish and the royal assent made stealing
a sheep punishable by death.[1]

In 1801, the year of widespread hunger, sentences
were passed at a single assize at Salisbury which were
to make six widows and 29 orphans. One of six men
hanged had been a highway robber, another a horse-thief
but the remaining four had all been sentenced for sheep-
stealing. That was a year of exceptional hunger and of
widespread unrest among the poor and fear among the
propertied and in fact most persons convicted of the
offence during the ninety years it enjoyed capital status

1 Anne Hughes, *The diary of a farmer's wife*, ed. Susan Beedell
   (Countrywise Books, 1964) p.70; *Journals of the House of
   Commons*, XXIII (1737-41) 572, 585, 690.

did not hang. More often they were reprieved for transportation. Even poor men convicted of stealing single
sheep were not returned to their families and neighbour-
hoods. Apologists for the eighteenth-century penal code
are apt to make much of the fact that most capital
sentences were not actually carried out but it is worth
bearing in mind the words which Jeremy Bentham put into
the mouth of a judge passing sentence of transportation:

> I sentence you, but to what I know not;
> perhaps to storm and shipwreck, perhaps to
> infectious disorders, perhaps to famine;
> perhaps to be massacred by savages, perhaps
> to be devoured by wild beasts. Away - take
> your chance; perish or prosper, suffer or
> enjoy; I rid myself of the sight of you.[1]

Nevertheless whatever the likelihood of reprieve, until
1832 men convicted of sheep-stealing even without any
aggravating circumstances could be, and some in every year
were, hanged. The notion that a man could be hanged
for stealing a sheep or a lamb has not only passed into
a popular saying but made a strong enough impression on
the village mind for some traditions to rest on the
assumption that sheep-stealing remained a hanging offence
long after the repeal of 1832.[2]

Official statistics do not make the measurement of
sheep-stealing committals on a national basis possible
before 1810. Between that year and 1840 committals in
England and Wales averaged 207 a year. In terms of per
100,000 of the population, peak years were 1817, 1827,
1830 and 1837. For the eighteenth century the much less
reliable conviction statistics are available for some

---

1 *Hampshire Chronicle,* 30 March 1801; quoted in Alan G Shaw,
   Convicts and the colonies (Faber, 1966) p. 57.

2 See for example Bob Copper, *Songs and southern breezes*
   (Heinemann, 1973) pp.11-20 where a story is recounted which
   took place at the end of the nineteenth century and yet ends:
   'and the penalty for sheep-stealing in the old days was
   hanging by the neck'.

circuits: the Western from 1770 to 1818, the Norfolk
for the same years and the Oxford from 1799 to 1818.
These show an interesting consistency with evident
peaks in 1782 and 1786 and a great vaulting leap in
1801.[1] Dr Hay's findings for Staffordshire also show
the peaks of 1786 and 1801 but in 1783 rather than 1782
and for the earlier part of the century in 1742/3,
1766/7 and 1775.[2]

It is doubtful whether the repeal of the capital
sanction in 1832 had a marked effect on prosecution
levels. In theory reluctance to begin a process which
might take a poor man to the rope, might have led to
under-prosecution of known offences, while the removal of
the sanction could have reduced this disinclination.
This was the argument of the criminal law reformers but
official statistics show 1231 committals in the five
years leading to 1832 and 1320 in the five years
following. Committals for horse- and cattle-stealing
covered in the same repeal actually declined in the
second five year period.[3]

Not infrequently contemporaries expressed the view
that for the most part sheep-stealers were hunger-driven
men rather than hardened criminals. The peak years
coinciding as they do with years of high bread prices
and widespread shortages support this. Those of 1766/7,
1782/3, 1801, 1817 and 1830 all coincide. It is a
reasonable assumption that hungry men steal when food

---

1   Statistics after 1818 are taken from the annual returns but
    up to that date from the appendices to the *Report from the
    Select Committee on the Criminal Laws*, BPP, 1819, Cmd. 585,
    viii.

2   Douglas Hay, 'Crime, authority and the criminal laws in
    Staffordshire, 1750-1800', unpublished PhD thesis,
    University of Warwick, 1975, p. 72.

3   K K MacNab, 'Aspects of the history of crime in England and
    Wales between 1805 and 1860', unpublished PhD thesis,
    University of Sussex, 1965.

prices in general are high: while 'professionals' would
be likely to increase their activities when meat prices
were high. The peak of 1837 is the only one which
clearly coincides with a widespread scarcity of fat
beasts.

In one of the few surviving folk-songs about sheep-
stealing, the stealer was 'most wonderful poor'[1] and
in a work of 1781 we read:

> Poverty alone can induce men to be guilty of
> it; and it is very hard that the same severity
> should be inflicted upon the wretched sheep-
> stealer, whose hunger and the cries of his
> family have driven him to the commission of
> this crime, as upon the hardened highwayman,
> who robs to support himself in luxuries, and
> to dissipate it in the most abandoned pursuits.[2]

In instances motivated by poverty several things might
generally be expected to have been true: i) the accused
was not a member of an organised gang; ii) one or perhaps
two sheep were taken rather than significant numbers;
iii) that there was no record of a criminal past. In
addition it would confirm results if sheep-stealers could
be shown to have been men of the age at which family
support pressures were likely to have been heaviest.
A preliminary investigation of 1834 suggests this last
may have been true. In that year 62.7 per cent of
committals for sheep-stealing were of men between 22 and
40 years and only 21 per cent younger than 22. For all
crimes the figures were 44.9 per cent and 41 per cent.
Female convictions were very rare.[3]

1   Albert L Lloyd, *Folk song in England* (Panther edition, 1969)
     p. 239.

2   George Parker, *A view of society and manners in high and low
     life* (2 vols, London, 1781) I, 162-3. *Commons Journals,*
     XXIII (1737-41) 572 (7 January 1740), 585 (14 January 1740).

3   Based on returns in *BPP*, 1835, Cmd. 218, xlv, *Criminal
     offences for 1834.*

Of 39 cases reported in sufficient details in the
Cornish press between 1811 and 1850, 29 involved the
stealing of only one sheep, nine of several sheep and in
one case it is unclear. In two of the 29 cases of single
sheep-taking, lambs were taken and kept alive and so
immediate hunger was presumably not the motive. In 25 of
the 29 no associates were mentioned. In the four cases
where associates were implicated, in one the relationship
between the two men is unclear; in another they were
'labouring men', perhaps work colleagues; in a third an
accomplice with a butcher's knife was seen but not taken;
in the last the pair were brother and sister. Only one
of the 29 seems to have had a previous record. Michael
Stevens, convicted in 1820, was described as a 'very bad
man' by the person he himself called on for a character
reference. At his execution he attributed his loss of
character to having been imprisoned before and 'hardened
in guilt'.[1]   One other was charged at the same time with
stealing clothes but the court accepted that he had
become deranged since the death of his wife.[2]

Several pleaded poverty in their defence. One of
these, a cottager on the common, said he had had no money
to buy food. Another spoke of being driven by 'extreme
distress' and for a third the man from whom he had taken
the sheep spoke on his behalf of his wanting 'the
necessaries of life'. Five had previous good character
pleaded for them and in several cases the description of
the discovered mutton as being cut up in 'an unbutcherlike
manner' suggests consumption rather than resale.[3]

1   *West Briton*, 8 September 1820.

2   *West Briton*, 5 August 1820.

3   *West Briton*, 2 April 1824, 3 April 1818, 28 March 1828.

During the debate on the repeal of the capital
act, the feeling that sheep-stealing was not usually a
crime of 'deliberate wickedness' was frequently and
widely expressed. It was rather a crime which might be
perpetrated without any 'combination' by a labourer in
temporary distress. In general the Cornish evidence
supports this view but there were nevertheless a number
of cases in that county and elsewhere where the motivation was clearly different: there is even more
uncertainty about the eighteenth-century evidence.
Dr Hay has written of a black market in mutton operating
in eighteenth-century Staffordshire and of butchers who
specialised in receiving stolen meat.[1] Alfred Peacock
has uncovered an East Anglian gang in the 1830s who had
an arrangement with local butchers for a rate of 10s
a carcass if the skin was cleanly removed and some
Bedfordshire sheep were so professionally skinned that
they were thought to have been destined for the quality
London market.[2]

Butchers appear as accomplices in four of the Cornish
cases and one was strongly suspected in a fifth. Elsewhere in the west country they also appear. John
Uppington, convicted at Ivelchester in 1799, was a
master-tailor, schoolmaster and parish clerk but even
his varied skills were not thought up to the skill of
butchering when he was caught and a butcher named Westcott
was named as an accomplice although insufficient evidence
could be produced to secure a conviction. A Devon

1   Douglas Hay, 'Poaching and the game laws on Cannock Chase'
     in Douglas Hay, Peter Linebaugh, John Rule, Edward Thompson
     and Calvin P Winslow, *Albion's fatal tree: crime and society
     in eighteenth-century England* (Harmondsworth: Penguin Books,
     1977) p. 205.

2   Alfred Peacock, 'Village Radicalism' in John P D Dunbabin,
     Rural discontent in nineteenth-century Britain (Faber, 1974)
     pp. 43-4.

butcher was hanged in 1798 and another charged along
with a blacksmith in 1801.[1]

Unless for poaching, it is not easy to uncover
individuals with recurrent criminal acts in their past.
But as C D Brereton, one of Edwin Chadwick's most
persistent critics and totally opposed to the idea of
establishing a rural constabulary, pointed out:

> In cities the majority of thieves exist in
> gangs, practice fraud by profession, and live
> by a constant series of depredations . . .
> criminals in the country only occasionally
> once or twice a year steal a sheep, pig, corn,
> hay, wood, turnips, poultry as the case may be.[2]

One of the Cornish committals for stealing a single sheep
had a previous conviction. Another in 1818 had been in
gaol before but as his character witness explained: 'it
was not for felony, but for smuggling' and he was a man
of good character. Perhaps not so was the butcher caught
in the act on Hackney marshes in 1742. He had been
burned in the hand thirty years before for a similar act
(before the capital sanction) and two of his sons had
already been transported for highway robbery. Others
confessed at their trials to having been regular sheep-
stealers or to other forms of robbery. Charles Rudman
confessed at Salisbury in 1801 that he had been taking
sheep and calves for many years; he was also suspected
of murder. Issac Box, convicted at the same assize, had
been extensively engaged in sheep-stealing and had twice
committed burglary and once highway robbery, besides
innumerable thefts of poultry. In 1806 a shepherd and
labourer convicted together in Salisbury were represented

1   *West Briton*, 15 August 1816, 3 April 1818, 27 March 1829,
     13 August 1830, 5 August 1836; *Sherborne Mercury*, 18 February
     1799, 16 April 1798, 30 November 1801, 13 April 1742.

2   C D Brereton, *A refutation of the First Report of the
     Constabulary Force Commissioners*, pp. 72-3.

as having been engaged in the practice for many years
and received the death sentence. Levi Chivers, indicted
at the same assize in 1815, had stolen 153 sheep from
five different parishes and in one parish alone from
five different owners. [1]

Taking sheep in such numbers was clearly rustling
for resale and, even if discovered in only one offence,
men taking them cannot be assumed hunger-motivated.
One committed to Maidstone Gaol in 1742 had driven 37
sheep and two lambs to Smithfield. A farmer's servant
stole 25 ewes near Winchester in 1773 and sold them
for £15 at Petersfield Fair. 'Farmers should therefore
be very cautious of whom they buy such small parcels of
sheep, even at public fairs', cautioned the *Hampshire
Chronicle*. William Rowe, executed in Cornwall in 1818,
had stolen ten sheep on one occasion and fifteen on
another. He sold them to a market butcher for 22s each.
In 1828 the taker of 61 sheep from a fold of 554 offered
them for sale at Devizes Fair the following morning.
Such examples could be multiplied and clearly an
approaching fair offered tempting resale possibilities. [2]

Sheep-stealing by gangs was widely reported. A man
convicted at Winchester in 1773 of stealing wheat,
confessed to having been one of a gang 'of desperate
villains' who had stolen many sheep in that area. In
the following year Hampshire was still being troubled by
a gang of horse and sheep-stealers who were killing

1   *West Briton*, 14 August 1818; *Sherborne Mercury*, 13 April 1742;
    William Dowding, *Fisherton Gaol: statistics of crime from 1801
    to 1850* (Salisbury, 1855) entries for 1801, 1806, 1815.

2   *Sherborne Mercury*, 30 November 1742; *Hampshire Chronicle*,
    18 January 1773; *West Briton*, 14 August 1818; Dowding,
    Fisherton Gaol, entry for 1828.

sheep and leaving their skins, heads and entrails in
the fields. Several committed to Ilchester gaol in 1799
were supposed to belong to a gang who had been taking
sheep for some time. A gang of seven, of whom four,
all local people, were taken in Devon in 1742, had
stolen cider-apples, linen and lead as well as three fat
sheep. Thomas Vardy, convicted at Dorchester in 1788
for returning from transportation to which he had been
sentenced four years previously for sheep-stealing, had,
since his return, 'terrorised' the village of Glanville
Wootten with a 'gang of villians'. Dartmoor and Exmoor
were in 1801 experiencing 'to a most atrocious extent':
'The business (for as such in some parts of the county
it seems to be almost exclusively practised) of sheep
stealing'.[1]

These instances refer to persons grouped in a
lasting sense for the committing of criminal acts but
sheep-stealing groups were often more informal
associations of family or neighbourhood. Thus in 1829
in Cornwall four men, two of them brothers and one a
butcher, met to plan a sheep raid. They took four rams
but on pursuit one of the brothers fell into the sea
and drowned. The involvement of the butcher suggests
that they were intending resale of the meat but at
their trial there was no suggestion that they had
combined other than for this one escapade. They cannot
be described as a gang in the sense of an organised
grouping of criminals. A 'gang' suspected in Somerset
in 1801 consisted of a man and his three sons and two
brothers. Three seamen who took a sheep in 1815 were
father, son and son-in-law, while Robert and Betsey

---

1   *Hampshire Chronicle*, 18 January 1773, 24 January 1774;
     Sherborne Mercury, 22 July 1799, 2 February 1742, 14 January
     1788; Charles Vancouver, *General view of the agriculture of
     the County of Devon* (London, 1808) pp. 366-7.

Percy, convicted in Cornwall in 1842, were co-residing
brother and sister. Similar pairings took sheep elsewhere, although more commonly a wife than a sister;
Charles and Ann Miners, convicted at Salisbury in 1817,
were condemned by Charles's diary in which he had
actually recorded: 'About home and night to L.mill after
NARB and W prig'd two Sh'P'.[1]

Rarer than cases of taking for consumption or for
immediate resale but not unknown were cases of stocking
farms with stolen livestock. When in 1776 a Devon farmer
was charged with cattle stealing, investigation revealed
that he had rented a farm at £100 per annum and that
among his stock were six stolen horses and more than a
hundred stolen sheep taken from different persons and
places. A Herefordshire farmer who hanged himself in
Gloucester gaol in 1785 had stocked a farm with over 60
head of sheep and cattle stolen from different parts of
the country. A Cornish farmer was fortunate in 1849
that a jury could not agree when he was observed in the
act of putting a strange lamb to one of his ewes.[2]

Clear cases of 'rustling' apart, the adding of
stolen sheep live to existing flocks directs attention
to the matter of strays. Some evidence suggests that
in the minds of country farmers and shepherds there was
a distinctively permissive attitude when it came to
allowing strays to remain with their flocks. The
execution of a thirteen year old boy at Ilchester in
1786 dramatically illustrates this. Edward Wiatt had
been convicted along with another man of going into his
own father's field and taking away what was in fact a

1   West Briton, 27 March 1829; Sherborne Mercury, 29 June 1801;
    West Briton, 7 April 1815; Cornwall Gazette, 25 March 1842;
    Dowding, Fisherton Gaol, entry for 1817.

2   Hampshire Chronicle, 18 March 1776; Sherborne Mercury,
    4 April 1785; Cornwall Gazette, 30 March 1849.

stray, although he claimed not to know this but believed
that it belonged to his father: 'as it was a sheep that
had strayed from its own flock, into his father's from
whence he took it'. The *Sherborne Mercury* made the lad's
fate the subject of lengthy editorial comment:

> As sheep stealing appears to be a very growing
> evil, it would be well if the rigour of the law
> were more generally understood . . . Boys and
> servants observe strangers among their flocks,
> and as by growth in size and of wool they are
> not to be discovered, the masters or parents
> take them as their own. This is observed by
> the whole family, who thinking it easy are
> induced to hire small farms or connect them-
> selves with those that have such - and to
> cause strangers from flocks in a variety of
> ways which an open country is easy to be
> effected and success prompts repetition.

Masters and parents should refrain from setting such a
'dreadful and often fatal example'. Instead they should
regularly search their flocks and advertise strays: 'so
that it may be impressed upon the minds of servants and
boys that the detaining or secreting the strayed sheep
may be a means of much trouble and distress'.[1]

In the following year a farmer in the west country
was convicted of stealing seven sheep found in his flock.
He was worth £200 per annum and declared he had had no
intention of taking them and indeed to have been in the
act of driving them back when they were discovered to
be another's property. One Wiltshire farmer was later
remembered as having encouraged his shepherd to add
others on the way when driving flocks to market. Such
instances may lie behind the attitude which seems to be
revealed in the oral traditions recorded by Bob Copper,
W H Hudson, Alfred Williams and others in which sheep-

1   *Sherborne Mercury*, 24 April 1786.

stealers tend to figure more in the 'old rogue' than
the 'damned villain' category.[1]

Public sympathy for a poor man driven to steal a
sheep and suffering for it the extreme penalty of the
law does not in itself imply that sheep stealing was a
'social' crime in the sense of being popularly
sanctioned any more than does a permissive attitude
towards strays. Hudson's informant, an old woman of
94 when he spoke to her in 1910, thought hunger made
men indifferent to hanging and recalled one man hanged
at Salisbury who having a starving wife and children
had been 'maddened by want'. But this is excusing not
approving.[2] More difficult are the fuzzy areas where
shepherds' customary rights may have been involved.
A young shepherd was convicted at Oxford in 1832 of
killing and stealing a young lamb. The farmer had
discovered a skin and found the lad's mother cooking
the lamb. The shepherd argued that it was the custom
for shepherds to have small lambs that died. This was
accepted by the court but it was found that the lamb
had not died but had been killed.[2] Such customs
would have been very regionalised. None are mentioned
in the standard accounts of William Marshall. In fact
in other areas, not perhaps surprisingly, the shepherd
was encouraged to strive to keep small lambs alive
rather than let them die. In Herefordshire at the end
of the eighteenth century shepherds were paid a crown
piece at the birth of the first lamb towards the end
of February: 'We doe always doe soe for fere manie
lambes shoulde die as may happen iff wee doe not doe
soe', recorded a farmer's wife. Her shepherd certainly

1   *Sherborne Mercury*, 9 April 1787; William H Hudson, *A shepherd's
     life: impressions of the south Wiltshire downs* (Methuen,
     1910) p. 236.

2   Hudson, *Shepherd's life*, pp. 234-5.

did not have any perquisite right to dead lambs for she
also records that when her husband gave the shepherd and
the carter a ram killed in a thunder storm, they had not
had 'fresh meate to their platters for manie months'. [1]

Clearly sheep-stealing cannot be regarded as a
social crime in the sense that smuggling, wrecking or
poaching can. These were endorsed by the community in
most if not all cases. They were not actions considered
in themselves 'criminal'. Sheep-stealing was, although
the specific circumstances of its committal might in
instances bring popular approval as well as sympathy.
Such occasions might be those on which sheep were taken
or killed as acts of protest against persons who had
offended the community. In this sense of popularly-
approved act of protest or revenge, sheep-stealing
could in some instances be viewed as 'social' crime.
David Jones, who has made a study of incendiarism in
East Anglia in the aftermath of the rural labourers'
revolt of 1830, includes the stealing of livestock
along with incendiarism, poaching, animal-maiming,
machine-breaking and the sending of threatening letters
as 'traditional' forms of rural protest and argues that
only further research can reveal to the historian when
'crime' became protest. [2]

The protest nature of many acts of arson speaks
for itself although doubt might remain as to whether the
resentment expressed in flames was individually or
collectively felt. Sheep-stealing is less obviously

1   Margaret K Ashby, *The changing English village* (Roundwood
     Press, 1974) p. 273; Hughes, *Diary,* pp. 141, 167.

2   David Jones, 'Thomas Campbell Foster and the rural labourer:
     incendiarism in East Anglia in the 1840s', *Social History,*
     I (1976) 5, 11.
     On definitions of 'social crime', see John Rule, 'Social
     crime in the rural south in the eighteenth and early nine-
     teenth centuries', *Southern History,* I (1979) 135-53.

a protest action. However a growing body of evidence
suggests that in many instances it was of this nature.
Alfred Peacock has suggested that criminal actions of a
protest kind reached epidemic proportions in East Anglia
after the revolt of 1830 when, according to Hobsbawm and
Rudé, farm labourers 'waged a silent, embittered vengeful
campaign of poaching, burning and rural horror'. Peacock
has further shown that sheep-stealing was prominent among
such activities. In several cases recorded by him, only
choice portions of the beast were removed: 'skin, fat and
entrails were left as an awful reminder of the power of
the labourers'. He misleads us a little here. There are
other explanations for leaving the head, skin and entrails.
Basically it was good thieving. Discovery of concealed
skins was one of the commonest causes of detection. The
inquiry which had first led to the passing of the capital
act in 1741 had learned that many stealers came in the
night: 'killing great numbers of sheep . . . and stripping
off their skins, and then stealing the carcasses of the
sheep so killed, but leaving their skins behind to prevent
discoveries'. It also refers to cutting open sheep and
stealing 'their inward fat' and leaving the rest of the
carcass behind. The tallow, the fine fat around the
kidneys, had a high value to weight ratio and was easily
disposed of. [1]

Peacock is on stronger grounds when he examples the
posting of defiant notices, such as that affixed to a
Bedfordshire gate in 1836:

> Sir, your mutton's very good
> And we are very poor,
> When we have eaten this all up
> We'll then come and fetch some more. [2]

---

1   Peacock, 'Village radicalism', pp. 40-4; Hobsbawm and Rudé,
    Captain Swing, p. xxiii; *Journals of the House of Commons,* XXIII
    (1737-41) 572, 585; Hay, 'Crime, authority and the criminal laws', p.6

2   Peacock, 'Village radicalism', p. 44.

Another note was pinned to a gate in Cornwall in the
middle of a spate of sheep-stealing instances:

> Dear Sir William, do not weep,
> We've had one of your fat sheep,
> You are rich and we're poor.
> When this is done we'll come for more.[1]

It was not only in the 'sullen aftermath' of the
1830 rising that some instances of sheep-stealing can be
viewed as protest. An interesting sequence of events in
a Cotswold village in 1824 suggests a protest motivation.
At the harvest of 1823 an attack by an armed mob of
villagers had been made on an Irish harvest labour gang
brought in by several local farmers. One of the leading
farmers was Joseph Payne and on 10 February following,
two men, Robert Costin and James Hulet, were imprisoned
for sheep-stealing. On 13 February Payne's barn was
burned down and five days later a man was imprisoned
for attacking one of the watches at the fire. On
11 March the two sheep-stealers, Costin and Hulet, were
sentenced to be transported for life. On 16 March
Dickens Prigmore and George Costin (same surname as one
of the previously convicted sheep-stealers) were gaoled
both for firing Payne's barn and for sheep-stealing and
next day Francis Hulet (same surname as the other of the
first two sheep-stealers) was also gaoled both for the
fire and for sheep-stealing. Ultimately the two Costins
and the two Hulets were transported, Prigmore having
turned King's evidence. Clearly in such a case it is
difficult to separate the strand of sheep-stealing from
that of popularly supported incendiarism. The
perpetrators appear to have been the same men and the
target the same farmer who is known to have incurred

---

1   Alfred K Hamilton Jenkin, *The Cornish miner* (Allen & Unwin,
    1927) p. 300, note 94.

community resentment.[1]

Threats against flocks sometimes accompanied anonymous letters preceding food riots. Edward Thompson has provided two clear examples of this. The first from 1767 was pinned to a gate after a sheep had been stolen and it clearly shows that the stealing was intended as a protest against the farmer's charging of high prices for his grain:

Gentleman farmers

Farmers tack nodist from This time be fore it is to let

Be fore Christ mas Day sum of you will be as Poore as we if you will not seel Cheper

This is to let you no We have stoel a sheep, for which the reason was be Cuss you sold your Whet so dear and if you will not loer pries of your Whet we will Com by night and set fiar to your Barns and Reecks gentlemen farmers we be in Arnest now and that you will find to your sorrow soon

A Northamptonshire farmer received warning in 1800: 'If you dornt lower the greain whe will destroy all your farm with fire, whe will destroy all your sheep and whe will pull all your turnips up'.[2]

Reports of sheep-stealing from Sir William Yeo near Taunton in 1778 followed reports of other incidents on his estate, including his being beaten up by a gang of masked men. One strongly suspects grudge-motivation here. A witness from the same county was to tell a select committee in 1819 when asked about horse-, cattle- and sheep-stealing: 'in some instances, where people are

1   'A grave digger's diary' in John W Robertson Scott, ed.
     The countryman book (Idbury, 1948) pp. 156-64. The sequence
     of events described is on pp. 160-1.

2   Edward P Thompson, 'The crime of anonymity' in Hay et al, ed.
     Albion's fatal tree, pp. 281, 300.

excessively vindictive, they are very liable to have
their property stolen'.[1]

Historians have often suggested that the extent of
the pardons mitigates any description of the eighteenth-
century penal code as 'bloody'. Indeed the figures show
that few convicted sheep-stealers ended on the gallows.
But before we get carried away in praising the goodness,
kindness and mercy of the judiciary we should bear in
mind that the likely alternative sentence was long transportation. In the six years before the repeal of the
capital act (1826-31) when attitudes towards sheep-
stealers might have been expected to have been softening
rather than hardening, there were 935 convictions.
Of these, execution followed in fourteen cases. Of those
reprieved, however, 57.86 per cent were transported for
life; 14.43 per cent for fourteen years and 5.6 per cent
for seven years. There were evident fluctuations in the
ratio of executions to convictions with a greater likelihood of hanging in the eighteenth than in the early
nineteenth century:

Ratio of executions to convictions: Western Circuit[2]

1770-79	1:22.7
1780-89	1:12.9
1790-99	1:15.2
1800-09	1: 4.8
1810-18	1:14.9

The striking increase in the period 1800-9 is largely
accounted for by the single year 1801. No less than
sixteen out of nineteen executions on this circuit during
this period for sheep-stealing took place in that year.

1 *Sherborne Mercury*, 10 March 1788; *SC on Criminal Laws*,
   minutes, p. 105.

2 Statistics for the Western Circuit from the appendix to
   SC on Criminal Laws, appendix 9.

Official statistics for England and Wales show a
noticeable decrease in the likelihood of hanging in the
years leading up to the repeal:

Ratio of executions to convictions: England and Wales

7 years ending 1817   1:32.5
7 years ending 1824   1:21.1
7 years ending 1831   1:61

In his brilliant study of the working of the law in
eighteenth-century England, Dr Hay has stated that the
grounds for mercy were ostensibly that the offence was
minor, that the crime committed was not common enough to
need an exemplary hanging or that the convict was of
good character.[1] The grounds for choosing the victims,
for that is the truer way of looking at the problem, may
reasonably be presumed to be the obverse of these. Hay
has convincingly demonstrated that pleading poverty
alone was insufficient for reprieve. It needed to be
accompanied by strong testimony of good character. He
has also shown that, in the few instances where they
stole property of sufficient value, the well-to-do might
find their very affluence hurrying them to the gallows
so that the poor might continue to believe that all were
equal before the law. Thus in sentencing a prosperous
sheep-stealer in 1787 the judge remarked that the law
was tolerant of the trials of poverty but a 'rich rogue'
who stole under the mask of a fair and upright character
and was able to make depredations without being suspected
was not to be guarded against and was therefore more
culpable than a poor man who committed a criminal act
through real want.[2]

1   Douglas Hay, 'Property, authority and the criminal law' in Hay
     et al, ed. *Albion's fatal tree,* pp. 43-4.

2   Hay, 'Property, authority and the criminal law', p. 44.

The case of Henry Penson of Teignmouth in Devon is
interesting. A fifty-year old farmer owning a large
tract of land, he was indicted in 1801 for stealing a fat
sheep belonging to one of his tenants. Parts of the
carcass and skin were found badly concealed on his
premises and he offered a £500 bribe to the arresting
officer to let him escape. At his trial the court was
crowded and in his defence Penson argued the
improbability of one so well-off as himself stealing a
sheep and claimed that the skin had been 'planted'.
He could supply no alibi and when invited to call for
character witnesses could produce only a servant girl
who had been just three weeks in his employ. The jury
found him guilty with unusual dispatch. In delivering
sentence the judge lamented that a man though 'rolling
in affluence' could not refrain from 'violating the
property of his neighbour'. The verdict gave 'the
greatest satisfaction' to a crowded court. So
unpopular did the friendless Penson seem to have been
that it crosses the mind that he might have been 'framed'
by the planting of the skin. However his broadsheet
confession survives and concludes with a not-unexpected
plaudit to the English law:

> The excellency of the English constitution
> in its impartial awards of punishment must
> excite the admiration of all who see the
> rich culprit, whose crime was aggravated
> by the circumstance of his wealth, bend to
> an equally ignominious death with the
> meanest criminal.[1]

Other victims of the rope fit in well with Hay's
suggestions. Two executions on the western circuit in
1786, one of a thirteen year old boy, took place in a

[1]   Broadsheet in Exeter City Library and account in *Sherborne
       Mercury,* 20 April 1801.

year when sheep-stealing was prevalent enough to draw
out editorial comment in local papers. One of these
two, Tom Roberts executed at Bodmin, was clearly
selected to serve as an example. The unfortunate man
was of previous good character and had not even been
concerned with the actual taking of the sheep, although
he admitted being privy to the crime. Leaving a wife
and four children, he went bravely to the gallows begging
bystanders to take warning and not meddle with their
neighbours' property. At that time seven men were in
the county gaol awaiting trial for sheep-stealing. [1]
William Rowe, executed in 1818 also in Cornwall, was a
more obvious candidate for the fatal tree. He had stolen
25 sheep and the magnitude of his crime was compounded by
a previous conviction, although that had only been for
smuggling. In passing sentence, attention was drawn to
the extent to which sheep-stealing had been taking place
in the area. [2] The desire to make exemplary sentences
was especially evident in 1801 when in the Western
Circuit sixteen of the nineteen executions for the
offence carried out in 1800-9 took place in that one
year. It was a year of such widespread food-rioting
and industrial discontent in the south-west that an
historian has recently written of the 'revolt' in the
south-west. [3] Other examples confirm the 'choice' of
victims. Michael Stephens, executed in Cornwall in
1820, was of proven bad character with previous convictions. So too were Charles Rudman and John Partingall,
executed at Salisbury in 1800 and 1801. [4]

1   *Sherborne Mercury*, 24 April 1786.

2   *West Briton*, 7, 14, 21 April 1818.

3   Roger Wells, 'The revolt of the south-west, 1800-1801: a study
    in English popular protest', *Social History*, VI (1977) 713-44.

4   *West Briton*, 11 August 1820; Dowding, *Fisherton Gaol*, entries
    for 1800 and 1801.

Although it seems most likely that most sheep-stealers, especially in the hardship period of the first half of the nineteenth century, were hungry labourers rather than professional or even semi-professional criminals (a conclusion also suggested by a very high ratio of acquittals to convictions) it is also evident that the case study of sheep-stealing warns against making any simplified view of the causes of rural crime. There seem to have been very few cases in which sheep-stealers were not local people. There is little evidence of stealing by migrants although the 'floating' population of the bargees were said to take opportunities which presented themselves as they passed through the Midlands. Surprisingly the traditional villain of the countryside, the gipsy, figures hardly at all. This so surprised W H Hudson that, when he researched the local press for *A shepherd's life,* he recorded what sounds almost like disappointment:

> In reading the reports of the Assizes from the late eighteenth century down to about 1840, it surprised me to find how rarely a gipsy appeared in that long, sad, monotonous procession of 'criminals' . . . for stealing sheep and fowls or ducks or anything else.

He suggested that perhaps they were simply too skilled to have been caught and reported a communication from the *Salisbury Journal* for 1820 which claimed that gipsies would bury stolen sheep deep in the ground and then make their camp fire over the spot. If the sheep were not missed they could later return to dig it up.[1]

---

1   *First Report of the Commissioners on the best means of establishing a Constabulary force . . . in the counties, BPP,* 1839, Cmd. 169, xix, p. 3; Hudson, *Shepherd's life,* pp. 269-70, but see *BPP,* 1839, xix, p. 17, where many of the gipsies around Salford were said to have been sheep-stealers.

Hay has suggested that much sheep-stealing in the
Black Country was done by persons for whom stolen mutton
was a regular part of family diet over a period of years.
Such men stole with great caution and never in large
quantities. They were as likely to have been nailers,
potters or other industrial workers as farm labourers.
Such persistent dishonest thieves were sometimes
suspected by their neighbours but managed to avoid
detection for years; Hay suggests that perhaps 200 sheep
in a decade might be accounted for in this way. It is
indeed important to keep in mind that first offence really
means first known offence. However, the nature of
sentencing for a capital offence, at very least long
periods of transportation, does not make it possible for
there to be recurrent convictions. Evidence of earlier
activities might come up in the proceedings but equally
it might not do so. I prefer to reserve judgement.
Eighteenth-century assize records survive only very
poorly for the western circuit and the nineteenth-century
evidence, although it clearly enough identifies hungry
men, stealers for resale and social and individual
protesters, has nothing to say about persistent stealing
for family consumption. Without doubt it was not
unknown but it is impossible to determine its significance
as a percentage of total offences. When, and if, such
offenders were taken, they had no incentive to confess
to previous offences when nothing was more likely to
mark them for execution than an admission of habitual
depredation on the propertied.[1]

---

[1]   Hay, 'Crime, authority and the criminal laws', pp. 71, 73-4.
See also Jones, 'Thomas Campbell Foster', p. 11: 'Certain
families, even sections of villages, virtually existed by
crime - a yearly saga of stealing wood, turnip-tops, hay,
food, farm animals and game'; and Brereton, *Refutation*,
pp. 72-3, of 1839: 'I have known many persons transported
from the neighbourhood in which I reside, but not one who
had not some ostensible and legal occupation, and most of
them were as constantly employed in that occupation as other
persons of the same craft.

As most of my evidence has come from the counties
of the Western Circuit, does this make my suggestions
only regionally valid? I have found few disagreements
with Douglas Hay's account of the crime in Staffordshire
but sheep-stealing in the northern moors and hills where
flocks roamed unattended over vast tracts might have
developed on a very different pattern from, say,
Wiltshire, where sheep were herded in the day and folded
at night. In fact the west-country offers an excellent
cross-section of sheep-husbandry for it includes not
only specialised raising areas like Dorset and Wiltshire
but areas like Dartmoor, Exmoor and Bodmin Moor where
sheep were kept in conditions little different from
those of other upland areas of the country.

The research for this paper was assisted by a grant from the
British Academy.

OUTSIDE THE LAW:

TUDIES IN CRIME AND ORDER

1 6 5 0 - 1 8 5 0

Edited by

John Rule

Senior Lecturer in Economic and Social History

University of Southampton

University of Exeter

1982

©   Department of Economic History

University of Exeter

1982

ISBN 0 85989 188 7